THE ULTIMATE GUIDE TO LEAD GENERATION FOR B2C BUSINESS OWNERS

STOP WASTING TIME ON EXPENSIVE, UNRELIABLE MARKETING AGENCIES AND START GENERATING HUNDREDS OF QUALITY LEADS PER DAY IN-HOUSE

DAN WARDROPE
POLLY BROWN

Acknowledgments

Many people have helped me with the compilation of this book, and I would like to thank them for all their hard work over the last few months of writing, compiling information and design.

Firstly, I would like to thank the FlexxDigital team as a whole for their excellent work during 2018. We've made a lot of progress this year, and I have huge plans for 2019 and beyond.

Individually, I would like to thank the following people (in alphabetical order):

- Polly Brown for helping me to write this book.
- Graham Connolly for his various contributions to the book, his extensive knowledge of Facebook marketing, and the skills and enthusiasm channelled into becoming FlexxDigital's new PPC Account Manager.
- Alan Cotter for his contributions to the book, his extensive knowledge of and skill with Unbounce, and all his work in making Flexxable become a reality.
- Emily Farrington for taking hold of the new executive assistant post at FlexxDigital and being a very welcome addition to the team.
- Ariana Fleischman for her skills as a video editor, blogger and assistant videographer, and for her excellent contributions to FlexxTV.

- Gavin Miles, for his passion and commitment, while being the go-to PPC Accounts Manager, his various additions to the book, and all the help he's provided to our key 32 clients. Lastly, for managing and optimizing the millions of dollars in ad spend over the years. I am very pleased to have Gavin as the new Operational Director for FlexxDigital.

- Robert Pugh for generating over 200 videos since starting at FlexxDigital, his ideas for video content, and his invaluable assistance with the creation of FlexxTV.

- Milo Radojevic for his contributions to the book, and his aptitude for getting new clients for the agency at FlexxDigital.

Contents

Introduction *My Story and Why I'm Writing This Book* ... 1
The Good News ... 5
What This Book Can Do For You ... 7

Chapter 1 *Getting Enough Good Quality Leads To Service Your Business* ... 10
Generating High Quality Leads After GDPR ... 10
The Future Is Here: PPC Marketing ... 18
The Miracle of Facebook Advertising ... 27
Using Google AdWords ... 36

Chapter 2 *Why Marketing Agencies (Or In-House Marketing Teams) Are Failing You* ... 44
Why Expensive Marketing Agencies Often Don't Deliver ... 44
If They Can't Do It, How Can I? ... 49

Chapter 3 *Expanding Your Marketing Team Efficiently* ... 54
5 Reasons To Hire A Graduate ... 58
The Test Tasks ... 64
Interviewing and Making A Decision ... 73

Chapter 4 *Building Facebook Campaigns for Great Quality Leads*..... 80
The Facebook Algorithm 80
The Facebook Pixel 89
How To Create Intrigue Rather Than Sell Your Service 93
How Advertorials Work 102
The Magic of Facebook Video 110

Chapter 5 *Creating a Sales Funnel For High Quality Leads* 126
Why Isn't My Website Converting? 126
The Power of Unbounce 129
Building Advertorials and Landing Pages 134

Conclusion *Learn To Fly* 140

Introduction

My Story and Why I'm Writing This Book

Hello. My name's Dan Wardrope, and I'm the founder and director of FlexxDigital Ltd, a specialised Lead Generation Agency based in the South of England.

Since I established FlexxDigital four years ago, it's become one of the leading players in online lead generation. It's a trailblazer in the field.

Over the last two years, I've spent close to $4 million on Facebook ads and have a portfolio bursting with multi-million-dollar clients. This money isn't from managing a client's advertising spend; it's all my own investment, from my own credit card, and 100% my own risk. As you can imagine, the pressure can be overwhelming because it's not just my reputation at stake. Everything is on the line - from my house, to my business, to my whole way of life.

From that $4 million, I have managed to generate $50 million in revenue for my customers.

My business has been doing well. So well, in fact, that demand now outweighs supply. Earlier this year, an idea began to form in my mind. If my company had done so well, couldn't I teach others to do the same?

In the following months, a subdivision of FlexxDigital started forming. I gave it a name - Flexxable. It was built as a sort of "education hub"; a teaching facility where I could help budding entrepreneurs who wanted to create an agency similar to FlexxDigital, but having trouble getting started.

Later, I branched out even further to help company owners who wished to establish an in-house marketing team and generate leads for themselves.

That's where this book comes in.

Day in and day out, I see the misery on my clients' faces when they hear the term "marketing agency". Many of them have worked their way through four or five, and have been taken in by the same poor marketing techniques again and again.

I share your frustration. I understand your doubts and concerns.

But I want to offer you something very different in both approach and results; I'd like to share my secrets with you. They're all within this book.

In this book, you'll discover the ultimate game-changer when it comes to securing customers and generating hundreds of low cost, high quality leads every single day.

You can do this in-house, with no headache and barely any technical knowledge. You'll never need to hire the services of a marketing agency ever again.

If this sounds too good to be true, well… I'm not a wizard. I can't wave a wand and fix all your problems from the get-go.

Forming an internal marketing team and generating your own leads takes hard work. You'll need the right mindset and a hunger to make tomorrow even better than today.

You see, before spending millions on Facebook ads, I struggled for years.

Like most people, I followed the conventional path. I went to school and then onto university to study chemical engineering. This was all with the belief that a good education would set me up with a good career and a happy life.

Unfortunately, there was a flaw in the plan.

I really struggled at university. The course was supposed to last for four years but, finding everything so difficult, I ended up doing five.

At this point, I should have cut my losses and quit chemical engineering. I didn't. I had worked so hard to get my degree that I felt I had to use it.

Ten years on, I found myself stuck in a job I loathed. There were times when I would lie in bed, staring at the ceiling, and dreading having to go to work.

Come January 2009, I was so desperate to change my life, I typed "How To Make Money Online" into Google.

Little did I expect this small act would take me on a six-year journey. Sitting in my bedroom, I read stories about being your own boss, and newsletters from the likes of Wealthy Affiliate University and Frank Kern. Inspired by lives far more glamorous than my own, I taught myself Pay Per Click marketing in the evenings after work.

Eventually, I found myself working for a "not for profit" company spending about $40k a month on Adwords. I was getting great results and introduced the business to Facebook advertising. Instantly, my management fee doubled.

For the first time in a long time, things were great. I was getting good money from this client, and I'd earned it. I was learning so much, spending upwards of $3000 a day on advertising, and making new discoveries every day.

Until things turned a little sour.

Unfortunately, the client started delaying their invoice payments. I was getting paid later and later each month until I was owed a vast sum of money.

I decided to cut my losses and moved on. When I next spoke to my mentor, he advised me to build a lead generation website and try my hand at selling leads for myself. With the knowledge I'd learned from running this client's account, I went to find the next big buyer.

Incredibly, I landed myself a whale. Within six weeks, I was making around $15,000 profit per month.

I hired an office and my first employee. Now, I have eight employees, millions of dollars in profit, and a life I only ever dreamed of, 10 years ago as a chemical engineer.

Not that my journey didn't have its fair share of bumps along the way. I made many mistakes, but I learned from every single one of them. Looking back, there's nothing I regret - taking on too many clients, making advertisements that bombed - because I took responsibility for my own choices, knuckled down and shaped my business into one that's generated 181,583 B2C leads in the last 12 months. I made the mistakes, so you never have to. And, in the process, I became a master. I accumulated and invented the tools you and your Marketing team need - both physical and mental - to achieve at the same level.

I want to make it my mission to help business owners - whether they be small, medium, or large - take their advertising and marketing in-house. Leads are the lifeblood of any business. I, myself, have felt the resentment that comes with putting your company's destiny into the uncaring hands of a third party and, frankly, it sucks.

The Good News

Using Facebook and AdWords used to be a headache.

Luckily, with the rise of the digital age, more and more companies are starting to branch out with online advertising. Facebook and Google have adjusted their advertising interfaces to make them easier to use. Within the last year, Facebook ditched the "Power Editor" component as its primary platform and incorporated the current Ad Manager setup.

Thanks to this alteration, you can now publish small changes instantly, and all your work is saved as you go.

Since Facebook came into the game, AdWords has seen a new competition that's seizing a large portion of the advertising scope with a clean and straightforward interface. Determined not to be left behind, they've rebuilt their system to compete with Facebook.

Though this may seem like a case of petty point-scoring, it means these advertising platforms are easy enough for any Joe Bloggs to use.

Part of this ease of use comes with the exponential growth of artificial intelligence. AI is making advertising easier, smarter and more efficient. Popularised in 2014, artificial intelligence-based ad buying helped remove the broken, laborious manual tasks of researching target markets, insertion orders, budgets and layers of analytics tracking.

The marketplace approach to buying and selling digital ads is now managed through intelligent tools that can make decisions and recommendations based on the desired outcome of any campaign. By now, Facebook and Google can offer a service where you create a catchy ad, and the platform will use a set of algorithms to find the most promising prospects. As little as five years ago, building campaigns and targeting were arduous tasks, best left to expensive "professionals".

How times have changed.

There's now no need to go to expensive agencies or rely on third parties for advertising. My mission, in this book, is to give you a template to run your own advertising campaigns and grasp destiny in your own hands.

What This Book Can Do For You

In this book, I will share with you:

- **The Ultimate Guide to Mastering Facebook.** Many businesses tell me that Facebook advertising doesn't work. Their product is too niche, or they're getting an incredibly low hit-rate for far too much money. But, the problem isn't that Facebook doesn't work, it's that businesses just don't know how to use it. For example, all the leads we sell have a 25-75% markup when we send them onto clients. Some of our clients have been buying leads off us for over three years. If they can make their business work with such a large lead budget, can you imagine the untapped profits of generating all your own?

  My guide to conquering Facebook will give you extensive, easily digestible instructions on how to plan, craft and hone your Facebook campaigns, leading to lead after lead after lead.

- **How To Quickly Build Profitable Campaigns Using Google AdWords.** Using Google AdWords can be difficult and expensive. Fortunately, there's a way to get your company at the top of the search engine while keeping costs down to suit your budget. I'll teach you how to use AdWords the simple way, maximising your ROI with minimal fuss and no lengthy "how to" manuals.

- **"Plug and Play" PPC Funnels and Landing Page Templates**. In my story, above, I explained how I spent years learning about PPC advertising and attending master classes. Over these years, I designed hundreds – if not thousands – of landing pages and Lead Gen funnels. And, finally, I've created a range of fool-proof templates that absolutely work. All you need to do is put in your product or service's essential information, upload, sit back and wait for the leads to roll in faster than ever before.

- **How To Continue Generating Leads After GDPR.** Re-written to reflect our booming digital age, GDPR pushes companies to think *smarter*, not harder. Although adhering to the policy seemed to be the end of the world for several global businesses, I'll show you GDPR isn't necessarily the end of marketing as we know it. It could mean your leads are of even better quality than before!

- **How To Hire And Manage New Employees.** With all the wisdom in this book, you could, technically, generate hundreds of leads a day entirely on your own. But, as the owner of your own business, I'm sure your attention is better focused elsewhere. I'm going to teach you how to hire bright young adults and graduates straight out of university, who can run a fantastic advertising campaign solo and make you a tonne of cash in the meantime. Not only are you building an asset for your team, but you'll also be fostering brilliant young minds... and paying them far less than you would a digital agency.

- **How Video Can Promote Your Business.** Facebook videos have the lowest Cost Per View of any social media ads - making them an affordable option for small businesses. Facebook 's algorithm values video content more than single or carousel images, because video can gain a higher impression share (therefore lowering the CPC). At Flexxable, we've recently started using video in a big way, branching out into a channel we've called FlexxTV. Although it's early days, the results have already been phenomenal, with plenty of clicks, Likes, and new customers.

Imagine if you could overcome expensive, unnecessary outside agencies, headache-inducing technical chaos, and underperforming advertisements once and for all. Forget about those shortcuts and start taking some smart cuts... playing right into the hands of guaranteed success.

Dan Wardrope
Lead Generation Connoisseur
Brighton & Hove, UK

Chapter 1

Getting Enough Good Quality Leads To Service Your Business

Generating High Quality Leads After GDPR

As we enter 2019, the General Data Protection Regulation (GDPR) is in full force.

Consumers see its impact every time a website asks for permission to collect cookies, while companies are being inundated with enquiries about personal information as users get to grips with protecting their data. Many companies have started calling several marketing strategies into question. Is cold-calling still legal? Is direct mail allowed? Threatened with a fine of either 20 million euros or 4 percent of their annual global turnover, some smaller organisations have **shut down completely**, stating they did not have enough resources for compliance.

Before GDPR, some companies were abusing their prospects' data with multiple cold-calls a day. There was no clear way to opt out of receiving these sales calls, so many people had to put up with a barrage of constant, irrelevant sales talk, coming in from all over the world. Eventually, these aggressive marketing methods came to a head with cases like Olive Cooke, a 92-year old woman driven to suicide by 3,000 charity requests in one year.

Since this well-documented crisis, a lot of dubious companies have been forced out of business by data-regulation policies beyond their ability to manage. One of the safeguards GDPR has put in place is a **documented limit** to the number of calls or letters sent to one individual, with an easy "opt-out" clause for any further use of their personal data. Negative impacts are now seen as cumulative, so lots of seemingly trivial inconveniences will be judged "significant" if repeated too frequently.

Which brings me to the good news.

Technically, GDPR hasn't curbed any form of marketing as much as it has made it more complicated. Cold-calling is still a legal way to generate customers, as is cold-email, direct mail, or any other form of targeting you can think of. Now companies are required to prove they act responsibly with personal data, public confidence in the sales industry has rocketed. In turn, a customer may be more willing to consider your particular product or service now they know their data is being handled correctly.

Rewritten to reflect our booming digital age, GDPR pushes companies to think smarter, not harder. Being more careful with how you handle data will help you streamline your database and isolate higher quality leads. It'll also increase the efficacy of all your marketing activities - as long as you're careful.

So, we come to the most important thing I'm going to stress in this chapter: it's all about creativity. Instead of CCing in or calling hundreds of people a day, blindly hoping they may be interested in your product, you need to start distributing informative, creative and tailored content that will make your prospects *want* to opt in. As said by Howard Luck Gossage, an advertising innovator during the "Mad Men" era, "Nobody reads ads. People read what interests them, and sometimes it's an ad."

Hand in hand with creative content is, of course, where you display it. Far from dampened by the new GDPR policy, social marketing is quickly striding up to its peak, stepping over the likes of television, radio and print.

Social media sites like Facebook, Instagram, and LinkedIn can integrate your ads into a potential customer's lifestyle in a way no other medium has managed before. It's a seamless method that allows your company to reach any type of person, of any age, from any city, with any interest, at any time. It also costs a fraction of any other form of advertising, netting huge profits for a successful campaign.

But don't just take my word for it. In the last year, we've learned the following stats about Facebook alone:

- 62% of adults in the UK use Facebook (that's 42 million users)
- There are 2 billion monthly active users on Facebook worldwide
- 76% of Facebook users visit the platform every day
- On average, people access Facebook 8 times a day, accumulating up to 50 minutes of user time
- 42% of Millennials (those born between 1981-1996) can't go for 5 hours without checking Facebook
- 62% of Marketers say Facebook is their main social media channel
- Facebook videos have the lowest Cost-Per-Click of any social media ads - making them an affordable option for small businesses.

If you, or any business, are willing to learn the **art of generating infinite leads through social media,** as I hope you are, you'll soon see *every single customer* you could wish for is on your digital doorstep. And the cost to reach 1000 people on Facebook comes in at the immense sum of...

$0.25.

For just $1, you could be targeting 4,000 people **a day**. With the right tailored content, hundreds of those 4,000 could become high-quality leads. As Brian Carter, author of "The Cowbell Principle", says: *"If you can't spare $30 a month, you shouldn't be in business."*

"Whoa, Dan, slow down," you may be thinking.

Look, I know it's overwhelming. But, you're reading this book so you can stop relying on expensive marketing agencies, and start generating hundreds of leads per day IN-HOUSE.

To make this possible, you need to look at *how* you're generating your leads, and *where* you're producing them. Let's look at other forms of advertising:

- **Television.** Ah, the Great God that is television advertising! I'll level with you - advertising on the television works. After the ad has been aired for 28 days, businesses, on average, will see a 5% sales increase. 43% of adults consumers say they're more likely to respond to a traditional TV ad than any other form of marketing. Fine.

  Is it for you? Well, it could be - if you have a huge advertising budget. For a 30-second slot on a mainstream UK channel, you could be paying anywhere between £1,000 - £32,000 ($1,300 - $40,000) depending on what time the advert airs. ITV, for example, charges up to £32,000 ($40,000) for an evening slot at 8pm. A less popular yet still prominent channel, like Channel 5, will charge £5,000 ($6,000) for a similar time. Once you've added the cost of an agency to negotiate the contracts, actors, writers, composers, equipment, etc., etc., you'll be spending the best part of £52,000 ($66,000).

I've found television is intrinsically connected to branding. So, for example, if you owned a furniture store, you'd be interested in making the name of that furniture store familiar to potential customers - to the point they'd be hard pressed to think of another, better, brand if they needed to buy a new sofa or a bed. While this sort of acute marketing has worked well for big brands such as DFS, smaller businesses looking for quick profits tend to be better suited to "direct response" marketing, where they can get an address, email contact and telephone number, and immediately dive in to make the sale.

- **Radio.** Out of the UK's total ad spend, about 3.1% is spent on radio advertising. As a general rule of thumb, advertising on the radio is charged at approximately £2.00 ($2.63) per 1000 listeners. So, in a morning slot, if 100,000 listeners are tuned in to a particular station, a 30-second spot will cost you about £200 ($263). Later on, between 10pm-5am (dead time), a station with 10,000 listeners will cost about £20 ($26).

Is it for you? Though it's cheaper than television, radio can rack up its own set of expenses, including a voice actor, composer, studio time, equipment, and so on. Costs can quickly accumulate, meaning a small business can easily spend £32,000 ($40,000) on radio advertising per year. It may not sound like much but, for many small-to-medium companies, this is a lot to spend without guaranteed results.

As with television, the effects are difficult to measure - meaning your ad could be on air for months before there are valid statistics to work with.

- **Print.** Print advertising has the curious contradiction of being an anomaly in comparison to other forms of advertising, but it still yields much the same results. Print ad spend declined steadily since 2007, with the $8.4bn investment trickling down to $3.34bn in 2017. Yet, it seems the public has a soft spot for print marketing. Valued for being less "interruptive" than television or radio, a reported 61% of adult consumers trust adverts in newspapers/magazines, compared to just 42% who prefer their sources to come from online.

  Is it for you? Once again, print advertising can be phenomenally expensive and works more as a brand-building tool than a way to generate instant results. Unless your budget is sky-high (a full-page black and white ad in *Vogue* can cost upwards of $100,000), your reach may extend only as far as the local newspaper. Within a few months (or likely a few weeks), you've exhausted your market in that area, and aren't generating any more leads.

  The next big clue is in print's dwindling ad spend. Down by $5.07bn over the course of 10 years, this significant decrease in funding is a mark of the ever-expanding digital age. According to the Audit Bureau of Circulations (ABC), print circulation across the entire market has fallen by 5% since 2016, while digital purchases have grown by 3.5%, and online readership for magazines and newspapers has leapt by 37%. For marketers, the switch from print to digital advertising has made life a lot easier - they can now accurately measure the number of ads, clicks, impressions and so on. With the ability to keep track of, amend, and split-test ads, the choice to transition from print to online advertising is a no-brainer.

- **Direct mail.** An amalgamation of print and cold-calling strategies, direct mail is a big industry within the marketing community. With a household response rate of 5.1%, a well-written letter can see a significant boost in sales for any product or service. Warmed by the tactility of receiving a physical envelope, audiences like it even more when the letter is personalised and in full colour - boosting their responses by 135%.

  Is it for you? As with print advertising, you have to be 100% sure of your messaging within direct mail. If you send out 1000 letters, by the time you've bought the envelopes, stamps, good quality paper, and printed in full colour, each letter could cost $4 - $5. If the message in that letter flops, your business could be out of pocket by $5000.

  It is possible to split-test with direct mail, but it's needlessly complicated, and you can't expect instant results. For example, you could have two different formats for the letter, using two separate phone numbers. Depending on which number receives the most calls, you can calculate which form was more successful with consumers.

  However, this method takes time. Direct mail is difficult to track, because people may not feel pushed to contact you straight away. Most will head straight to the web and make comparisons there, only calling in if they don't find a better offer. The split-test itself is just an outdated form of digital marketing -useful results could take weeks, whereas online you'll see results within hours.

If you've got an enormous advertising budget, hours to spare, and a marketing team that inspires nothing less than unshakeable faith within you, then you could generate many high-paying, quality leads using the strategies above. But, if you're looking to generate thousands of leads with an average size budget and minimal staff - as I hope you are - then the great heights of television and print advertising may be out of your reach.

But don't despair.

Incorporating social media advertising into your marketing strategy - if you haven't already - is one of the most significant leaps you'll take towards growing your business, generating infinite leads, and watching your profits soar. Best of all, I'm going to be with you, here in these pages, every step of the way.

93% of marketers use Facebook advertising, and 62% of small businesses say Facebook ads don't work. These businesses are **wrong.** Quite often, these companies lack the time, budget and knowledge to market themselves effectively.

I'm here to show you how to leverage a marketing strategy that will place your business in the prime position to generate prospects and convert them into leads.

I'm here to give you top tips on the best Facebook methods, and guide you through all the tricky bits that are woefully under-explained in any other book or blog (or, at least the ones you don't have to pay for).

I'm even here to tell you my TOP SECRET for ensuring **every single lead** you generate is legitimate and ready to buy.

Social media advertising is an opportunity, not a chore. Once you've honed in on your target audience (and I will show you how), we will work on crafting creative content to enchant your prospects. Creating fun, readable content and intensifying the extent of its reach with social tools can cultivate and refine your business. With the right personality, images, and message, you can send your offer soaring above your competitors'. It all depends on how you use what's right in front of you.

I'll teach you. Come on, let's go.

The Future Is Here: PPC Marketing

As a business owner (and a soon-to-be Master Lead Generator), you presumably know what PPC advertising is. In fact, you probably pay an agency somewhere an absurd amount of money to run your PPC advertising for you. Don't worry, that will soon change.

PPC, or Pay-Per-Click, is everywhere. If you've ever seen ads alongside your email inbox, or listed first in a search engine, or integrated into your Facebook feed, then you've encountered PPC advertising. Basically, PPC is an online advertising model in which marketers can display ads for products or services when consumers type relevant queries into search engines. Advertisers are only charged when a consumer clicks on their ad, hence the name "Pay-Per-Click".

A Brief History

To prepare for the future, it's vital to understand the past. PPC is a relatively new advertising model, with the first documented example taking place in July 1996 - only 22 years ago.

Back then, Google, the 80% giant of the search engine market, was merely the grub of a research project at Stanford University. The first example of Pay-Per-Click was launched on a web directory called Planet Oasis through a desktop application.

By 1997, more than 400 worldwide and local brands actively participated in PPC advertising. In 1998, GoTo.com introduced the bid system. Here, the advertiser could bid for ad position on keywords. The bid value would determine where the ad would turn up in a search result. The higher the bid, the higher the ad's priority.

At the turn of the Millennium, PPC advertising really started to make strides in the marketing world. In 2000, Google released an early version of the Google AdWords tool, a self-helping platform for sponsors. Advertisers could place ads for selected keywords and would only pay when the ad was shown. Google used the Cost Per Thousand (CPM) model, charging for every 1000 impressions - if a visitor viewed the ad, or if it was displayed on a webpage on the Google Network. I wish I was using PPC in those days!

Fast forward to 2007, when Facebook launched its own advertising platform. This allowed advertisers to target prospects by demographics and interests. By 2009, the internet had reached mobile devices. Google quickly tried to find solutions for mobile advertising by purchasing AdMob, a mobile advertising startup, for $750 million.

Just a few years later, in 2014, PPC advertising had really hit its peak - and the cost per click reflected this. Instead of just focusing on impressions, companies started to turn to conversion rate optimisation - the system that turns interested prospects into real-life customers – and to developing funnels and landing pages to maximise performance. Advertising spend was snowballing, with mobile spend up 98% year over year.

So, Where Are We Now?

In 2018, PPC remains a galaxy of opportunities. It is still one of the most profitable advertising and marketing channels, with a staggeringly high ROI compared to other, more traditional strategies.

PPC also yields immediate traffic and can help generate significant sales within weeks. You can easily set up a PPC campaign in about half an hour or so, whereas a television advert could take months. This "easy set up" feature is essential for new websites looking for exposure and visibility.

And, as soon as you have traffic, you can start to work on improvements. What does your site do well? What could it work on? Are the impressions converting to leads? If highly targeted traffic converts poorly, a usability reassessment can solve this. Sometimes, it's a case of a simple programming error or design oversight, like when an ad doesn't transfer to a mobile device.

On the other hand, if you created a site for your product or service without PPC, it could take months for traffic to ramp up to significant levels. A conversion problem in those three to six months could prove catastrophic for your business as, without adequate data, you may completely overlook the issue. PPC lets you fail fast *and sort the problem even faster.* A simple split-test with two versions of your ad online could save you hours of marketing grief, showing you immediately which variants work, which don't, and what needs to improve. It's both easy *and* cheap.

Which brings me to ***organic marketing***.

Many companies are drawn to organic marketing because it's free. They also have such unshakeable faith in their product or service, they embody the attitude, "build it and they will come". Unsurprisingly, these companies are bitterly disappointed when, six months later, they're up the creek without a customer in sight. It doesn't matter if you use the best materials. It doesn't matter if your product or service is superior to others of a similar type. If your prospects haven't heard of it, then they're not going to buy. Blogging on your website, or using great images, isn't going to help. When you post to your site, you rely on your site's visitors to find it. How many of these do you have? A post without readers is as pointless as a church without a congregation.

What Can We Expect By 2020?

At the top of its marketing game, PPC advertising has become simpler than ever. Gone are the technical setbacks and the notoriously tricky platforms. As PPC has grown in popularity, sites like AdWords and Facebook have made it easier and easier to get campaigns up and running, with all instructions in layman's terms. Hand over your campaign to a switched-on university graduate, and they'll be able to run the entire thing on their own while making you a sizeable profit.

As for creating websites and landing pages, this isn't the headache it once was. Saving you the wages of an expert web designer, online firms like Unbounce make the building of beautiful, professional sites a "drag and drop" experience. Branded as "The Conversion Platform For Marketers", you can explore the wealth of opportunities offered on their website: https://unbounce.com/.

The ability to build websites in under a day, coupled with the myriad of targeting opportunities available, means small to medium businesses have jumped on PPC advertising as a way to finally - and fairly - compete with the big boys.

Thanks to pricing models like Cost Per Acquisition (CPA, known as Conversion Bidding on Facebook), an advertiser's per conversion cost can be measured from start to finish, regulating how much is needed to convert someone from a prospect to a paying client. This is excellent for smaller businesses, or those on a budget, as they're only paying for the desired outcome. When capturing leads, for example, this is when a visitor provides vital information such as a name, email, telephone number and address. The more effective the campaign, the less you'll pay.

Facebook also has a feature called "Max Bid CPA", where you'll only pay what you can afford for a lead. For example, if you can only make leads work at $10, Facebook will look for leads where that's all you'll have to pay. You may not get as many as you'd like if you target the CPA too low, but it's an excellent little system for those without a huge ad spend.

I'll get onto the intricacies of Facebook and Google AdWord advertising momentarily. Before I do, I'd like to show you two companies who've managed to turn their brands into **multi-million acquisitions,** just from digital marketing.

Case Study 1: Dollar Shave Club

In just under six years, Dollar Shave Club has transformed from an idea between two men at a party to a global business that sold for $1bn in 2017.

DSC didn't reinvent the wheel. They took a boring, personal and genuine problem - shaving - and marketed it in a whole new way. Gone were the shots of smooth-faced celebrities playing high-intensity sports, or people tugging down their sleeves looking shame-faced. DSC's 2012 viral video used humour, cynicism, and - most importantly - *a great offer* to promote a reasonably pedestrian product. Razors, packaged and delivered straight to your door, for just $3 a month.

If you haven't seen the ad, now with 25 million views, you can do so on YouTube. Just type "Dollar Shave Club" into the search bar and click the first video, "Our Blades are F***ing Great".

Highlights include:

"Do you think your razor needs a vibrating handle, a flashlight, a back scratcher and ten blades? Your handsome-ass grandfather had one blade. And polio."

Although it was a high-risk marketing strategy (as going viral is mostly left to chance), 48 hours after the video launch, Dollar Shave Club received 12,000 orders. The surge in subscriptions was so vast, the website couldn't handle the traffic and crashed.

How Did They Do It?

Well-known brands spend millions a year promoting their products on television, radio and in print. Yet DSC managed to generate a cult-following in less than two days with a low-budget, 90-second long ad posted on social media. How?

They understood their audience. As you can see from the excerpt above, the ad definitely wouldn't appeal to everybody. It didn't need to. Mark Levine and Michael Dubin, the two founders, knew their target audience – people like them. So, the next step was to make a video *people like them* would want to see. As well as humour, their marketing strategy incorporated factors that transformed the company from mundane to extraordinary.

- **They offered a real solution.** Razors are expensive and, worse, they're forgettable. How many times have you lathered up and found your last disposable razor in the bin? Dubin and Levine combatted the problem by offering affordable blades delivered straight to your door, once a month. They didn't package the answer in fancy language. They simply stated what they were offering and gave prospects an open chance to opt-in.

- **They offered an experience.** As well as selling the product, Levine and Dubin lavished their customers with extras. Rather than send the purchase in waterproof packaging with a receipt stuffed inside, DSC's shipments arrive in a beautifully branded box, a welcome note, an explanation of the upgrade process and a monthly lifestyle newsletter, "The Bathroom Minutes". All this stuff is cheap to make and designed to keep the brand firmly fixed in the customer's mind. The consumer will really appreciate the extra effort - a bonus is just a bow that ties together an irresistible offer.

- **They welcome you to a select community.** The clue's in the name: Dollar Shave *Club*. You're not only buying a product; you're also joining an exclusive society. Tellingly, DSC never beg. They don't ever say, "Come and join us and be part of the gang!". Instead, they calmly place their offer on the table and leave the choices up to the prospect. The use of humour is the closest thing to a direct invitation - if you get the joke, you're one of us. If you're one of us, you could benefit from our product.

Case Study 2: Western Union

In direct contrast to Dollar Shave Club, Western Union has been around since 1860 and offers financial services rather than a tangible product.

Working in cross-border, cross-currency money movement, Western Union allows users to send money to others, pay bills, track transfers and to purchase Western Union "NetSpend" gift cards. In 2015, Western Union released a viral video, "American Dreamers," as part of a larger promotional raffle called "Western Union American Dream Sweepstake."

Interestingly, unlike the Dollar Shave Club, the "American Dreamers" video didn't mention the company's services. Instead, the in-house team of WU took an idea and developed it into an opinion-piece, travelling 13,779 miles across the United States and asking over 200 people whether they believed in the American Dream.

The result was 3 minutes of footage, with opinions ranging from mild scepticism to wholehearted agreement. Ending with the heartwarming message: "Western Union Believes in the American Dream for All," WU then offered audiences a chance to share their own thoughts about the American Dream and to enter the sweepstake, open for 11 months. Prizes included $35,000 towards a new car, $35,000 for a year of college funding, or a $65,000 down payment for a new home.

Between February 17 and June 30, 2015, the "American Dreamers" video captured more than a 1700% engagement rate on Facebook. The company's Facebook page tallied 735,824 impressions, 714 comments, 839 shares, 18,802 Likes and 31,112 engaged Facebook users. The sweepstake generated more than 13,000,000 eligible entries over 11 months and netted 5 prestigious campaign awards.

How Did They Do It?

- **They knew their audience.** Rather than promote a hard sell, WU took the opportunity to learn about their customers' hopes, dreams and aspirations. Interestingly, they didn't edit any of the comments to fit with their own agenda - the sceptics were proportionally represented alongside the optimists. Fans were drawn in by this message and sought to find out more about the brand.

- **They practised what they preached.** WU boldly stated "Western Union Believes in the American Dream for All," and their sweepstake followed through - all prizes were connected to the concept of the "American Dream". Customers could submit an entry form without making a money transfer, and those who did were automatically entered when sending money through the system. Essentially, the entire campaign was a bonus product - or the promise of one. Through engaging content and the temptation of life-changing prizes, WU built themselves as a useful, trustworthy and wholesome service.

- **They seamlessly integrated social and PPC marketing.** Like DSC, Western Union utilised the "One of Us" concept. Inviting prospects to share their stories on popular SM platforms such as Twitter and Facebook, half their marketing was achieved by word of mouth. Other promotional methods included online strategies such as banners, email, social media posts and frequent reminders on their website. Again, because they didn't use the "sell, sell, sell" tactic, prospects were more inclined to see the videos and posts as original content rather than disruptive advertising.

Dollar Shave Club and Western Union are just two examples of companies with stiff competition. Still, they managed to send shockwaves across the marketing industry using strategies deemed "inferior" by bigger, older businesses.

In 2019, social marketing is easier than ever. It makes sense, then, that businesses learn from past successes, take advantage of the opportunities available, and hone in on their audience as a way of generating supreme quality leads.

If all this sounds daunting, not to worry. The next section focuses exclusively on Facebook and how well it works as an advertising platform. All you need to do is turn the page.

The Miracle of Facebook Advertising

I've talked a bit about Facebook advertising before but, as we're hitting our stride and turning *you* into a Master Lead Generator for your business, it's necessary to delve into a bit more detail.

The success of Facebook is legendary. In 2011, Facebook had 500 million members, all generated within three years. Now, in 2018, 2 *billion* people log into Facebook every month. In August 2017, Mark Zuckerberg announced that his social network had passed a huge milestone - more than **1 billion** users logged into the platform in one day.

You know what else? 1.39 billion of these people access Facebook more often on a mobile than a desktop, and half a billion only ever access Facebook from their smartphone.

To put these numbers in context, let's check out the stats for other top social media platforms. These statistics are from TechCrunch, an online publisher of technology industry news.

- Snapchat has **255 million** monthly active users
- Twitter has **328 million** monthly active users
- Instagram has **700 million** monthly active users
- YouTube has **1.5 billion** monthly active users

Closely followed by YouTube, Facebook is still very much the giant across social media platforms. With user-numbers continuing to rise (250 million people joined the site between 2016 - 2017), it's likely Facebook will keep growing until it runs out of new people to sign up.

It goes without saying that Facebook is more than just a platform to share cat memes and prank videos. As the platform continues to expand, you've got millions of hungry people online, each for approximately 40 minutes a day, waiting for something to consume.

They're hungry for great content. They're craving new information or a solution to a problem. They're yearning for a small distraction - anything to put a smile on their face, to forget the office, or divert from the microwave carbonara they're having for dinner. Now the global population is at a peak, but as more people than ever suffer from loneliness, social media is a lifeline for those who want to touch the outside world. Within this massive pool of people are your future customers. You need to connect with them.

And it won't be easy - though I'll make it easier. Facebook will help you reach the right audience, but it's up to you to be relateable. Remember, prospects on Facebook don't want to be sold to. They want something that will make them think. Something that interests them, educates them, or makes them laugh. You need to be a jewel amongst the pebbles.

Facebook Video

In the past five years or so, video content has seen enormous growth. According to brandwatch.com, 6 out of 10 people prefer online video platforms to live TV. In 2015, 18-49 year-olds spent 4% less time watching TV while time on the popular video platform, YouTube, went up 74%.

But it's not just YouTube that's seeing a surge in viewer stats. Facebook has transformed into a video giant in its own right, spending $400 million to acquire LiveRail in 2014. With the help of the video advertising distributor, Facebook can place more than 7 billion video ads a month.

Now, in 2018, Facebook reportedly gets over 8 billion video views - that's 100 million hours watched- *every single day.* With 44% of small to medium business marketers promoting Facebook video content last year, more and more companies are taking this particular marketing strategy very seriously.

If your company hasn't invested in putting video ads on Facebook, there's a high chance your competitors have. As you now know, this puts you at a significant disadvantage.

With Facebook video, *brevity is the soul of wit.* 47% of the value of Facebook ads happens in the first 3 seconds. After the audience has settled in to watch the video, you need to keep your message quick and precise. According to Locowise.com, the optimum length for a Facebook video is 15 - 55 seconds and shouldn't be longer than 2 minutes, at risk of losing your audience.

Who's Your Target?

It seems a bit condescending to ask a business owner to think about their target market. After all, it's *your* product or *your* service, and you've made enough sales to keep afloat. You know that someone, somewhere, wants what you have to offer.

Unfortunately, lots of small to medium businesses think they know their target market, but fail to make their advertising appealing. Plenty of companies start with a target in mind, then forget as time goes on. Their advertising starts to trail off, becomes less focused, geared only towards the hard sell. And that's when the steady stream of customers comes to a halt.

Do you remember when I said that, out of the 93% of businesses who use Facebook as an advertising platform, 62% say it doesn't work? It's because they've lost sight of their audience. It doesn't matter if your ad is seen by 65 million people if the campaign has no concrete customer in mind. Trying to appeal to everybody is a sure-fire way to appeal to nobody.

Take a pen and paper, and sit down with a cup of coffee. Draw up an avatar of your ideal customer. This may take longer than you think! When I started, I thought that having a vague idea was enough but, when it came to putting pen to paper, I struggled.

Yet, when I had the specific facts in front of me, everything changed. My Facebook ads finally had a direction.

In your customer avatar, you should think about the following:

- Their gender
- Their age range
- Their location
- Their background
- Their marital status
- Their hobbies
- What films they like to watch
- What books, newspapers and magazines they like to read
- What other products/services they may be interested in
- Their fears and problems
- Their hopes, dreams and wants
- How your product/service solves their fears and problems and takes them closer to their hopes, dreams and wants

Once you've completed your avatar, you'll have a clearer idea of your target audience.

The targeting options on Facebook are amazing. Businesses can target prospects with Facebook ads by location, demographics, age, gender, and interests.

You can even go more in-depth and use Facebook to:

1. Get creative with life-event targeting (aka, a used car ad for someone who's just passed their driving test!)
2. Tap into recent purchase behaviour
3. Use custom audiences to nurture leads and loyalty (please note, GDPR now states you **must** have a user's consent before using their data to make a custom audience)
4. Create audiences that look like your own targets (lookalike audiences)
5. Layer targeting options to get outstanding granular targeting (granular targeting is when you cut out all the extra fluff!)

Here are some Facebook Demographic stats to get you a better understanding of who you can reach on the platform.

- 83% of women and 75% of men are on Facebook
- 88% of 18-29 year-olds have a profile
- 84% of 30-49 year-olds are active users
- 72% of 50-64 year-olds are on Facebook

- 62% of those aged 65+ have an account - a huge percentage considering only 20% have a LinkedIn page, and only 10% use Twitter
- 79% of users are university graduates
- 77% have finished secondary school
- 84% of adults who make less than $30,000 a year use Facebook, while 75% who earn $75,000+ a year have a profile
- 85% of Facebook's active users are from outside the US or Canada. India, Brazil and Indonesia have the largest percentage of Facebook users after America.

And if you're *still* worried Facebook may not reach the full extent of your audience, the platform can also show ads on Instagram (700 million active users), Facebook Messenger (1.3 billion monthly users) and Facebook Audience Network: an off-Facebook, in-app advertising network for mobile apps. Advertisers can display their ads to customers who are using mobile sites and apps *other* than Facebook, while still using Facebook's powerful targeting system. Using FAN can increase a campaign's reach by 16%.

Better still, Facebook advertising is no longer a complicated process, with Google AdWords following its example. Since its surge in popularity, and the hefty profit it makes (earning $52 billion in digital advertising revenue in 2017), Facebook advertising has gone to great lengths to make promotion possibilities simple enough for new starters or those with little to no technical knowledge.

I explain how to craft and hone perfect Facebook campaigns in Chapter 4 of this book, so please flick on ahead, if you'd like.

It's All About The Creative

And, by this, I mean how creative the ads are, and how creative *you* are when it comes to generating leads.

When I talk about Facebook Advertising, a lot of people say the leads they're generating are of poor quality. It's like seeing a trout pull the worm off the hook, then swim off into the reeds. It's very frustrating. And most people don't know what they're doing wrong.

They've made an advert with an eye-catching image and a strong headline. They've paid for a landing page with lots of fancy graphics and a call-to-action (CTA). Yet, when it comes to following up with those names, addresses and telephone numbers, they find the leads aren't qualified for the sale.

As far as the marketers are concerned, they've done everything right. So, they end up blaming Facebook.

There is a myriad of reasons why your ads may not be working, but Facebook as an advertising platform isn't one of them. Usually, it's something going on *beyond* Facebook, and beyond the prospect's initial click.

Let me illuminate.

Your ad is up online, with targeting scaled appropriately. The image you've used is one that'll generate a lot of interest, and you've got a headline between 4 - 13 words. Underneath, following Facebook's recommendation, you've got about 18 - 80 words about your product/service, but definitely less than 100. When the customer clicks the link, they're introduced straight to a box asking for their name and email address. If they scroll down, they may find a couple of testimonials and a short paragraph explaining what the company does, or what they're trying to sell.

Here's your problem. You're not giving your prospects enough information, and certainly not enough credit. It's like buying a car from eBay without asking for an MOT certificate and after being denied a test-run. You'd be making an enormous purchase almost wholly blind.

This is when you need to get creative. Once your Facebook ad has attracted the people unaware of your offer, it's time to move onto the second phase: consideration. This is where the magic happens. It's now your chance to educate the public on your product or service. You want to leave your visitors with:

A. More information than they've encountered before (making them better off)

B. A guarantee you're a legitimate company and not another scam

C. A hunger for your product/service. For the moment, the prospect can't imagine life without it

For this kind of funnel, I always use an advertorial.

Advertorials are advertisements written in the style of an article, allowing brands to tell their story in an engaging, informative or credible way. Noticeably, these advertorials **aren't trying to sell.** Or, at least, they don't look like selling is their primary concern. You can find some great examples of advertorials and sponsored content on BuzzFeed. For instance, Tylenol published this article promoting their Rapid Release Gels in 2017.

Using a blend of humour and popular culture, Tylenol cleverly takes a concept that seems irrelevant, but relatable, and makes it more relevant as the article goes on: time stands still when you've got a splitting headache. The audience is having so much fun, by the time they've hit the CTA and the "sell" at the bottom of the page, they don't feel like they've been forced into reading an ad. Like the Western Union "American Dreamers" Case Study in the previous section, Tylenol is working hard to build their brand with a certain kind of audience.

Of course, the advertorial needs to be in the kind of voice that best suits your company. You wouldn't advertise Funeral Plans with a set of memes and one-liners. But there are plenty of other ways to write an advertorial.

You could use:

- A newspaper-style article
- An opinion piece
- A quiz
- A video
- A listicle

Whatever you come up with, good advertorials focus on benefits, not features. To test this, remove all mention of your product/service from the final piece. If your advertorial still stands as an informative article that's relevant to your target audience, you've likely struck gold.

If your prospect reads the information then proceeds to give their details after the CTA, you can be sure they're a high-quality lead. As with your Facebook ads, always split-test and see which format or content resonates more with your prospects.

I'll tell you how to build the perfect advertorial in Chapter 5.

Now we've covered the indisputable stats and success of Facebook advertising, I'm going to tell you all about Google AdWords. If you haven't started advertising on Facebook today, I urge you to do so. You'll see the benefits in less than a couple of weeks!

Using Google AdWords

So, for those of you who aren't aware, Google AdWords is search-based advertising. Most of these ads aren't something people just happen to stumble across, as they may do in a social media feed. This person has sat down, thought about what they want, and typed it into Google's search bar.

I'll give you an example. Say you were a bit down in the dumps, and you wanted something you thought would make your life better. You type "sports car" into Google.

This is what comes up:

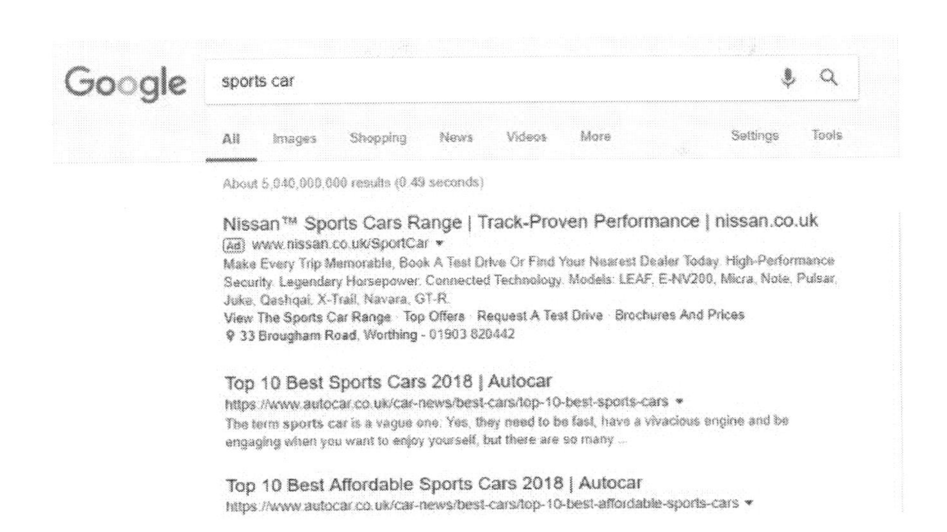

Right at the top is Nissan's page, with the word "Ad" next to the URL. Nissan has paid for this to be there, and the free (organic) searches are underneath.

You don't know if you fancy a Nissan, so you click on the organic search directly underneath: www.autocar.co.uk.

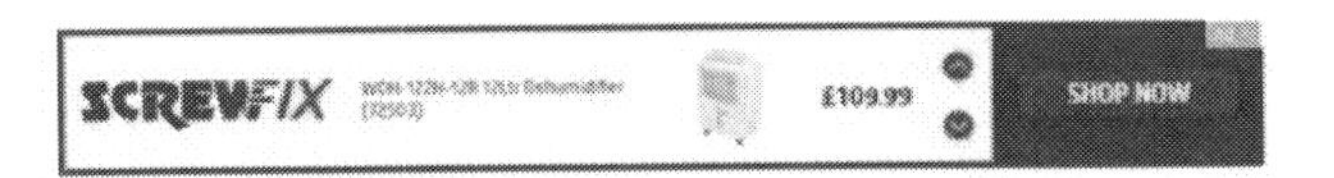

Top 10 best affordable sports cars 2018

Owning a sports car need not break the bank – here's our choice for the top ten affordable sports cars

You're greeted by this page. Immediately, you notice two ads on the screen - one from Screwfix, and the other from HP. Although neither has anything to do with sports cars, your butterfly mind is immediately attracted to the technology HP is offering.

This advert is served by Google's AdSense programme, where companies bid for ad space on other businesses' websites.

You click on the HP ad, and come to this.

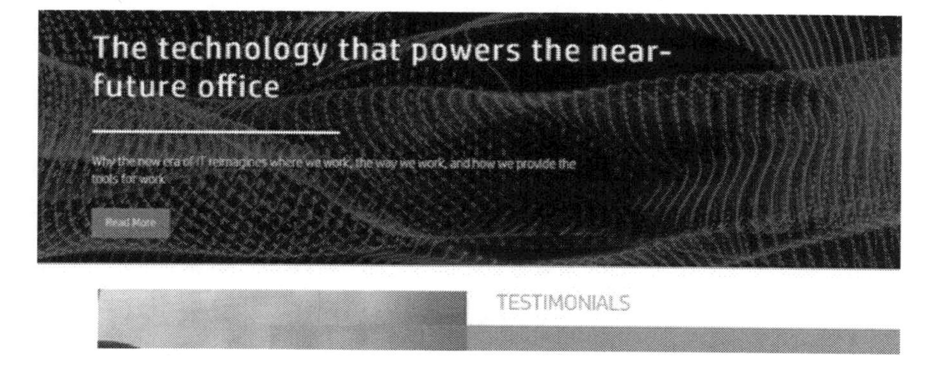

So, now you have three choices. You can read the testimonials for an unknown product, read more about the product itself, or leave the site.

HP knows this isn't an impulse purchase, so invites you to "Read More" in the CTA rather than demands "Buy Now".

You can then download an online catalogue about the products and its benefits. If you're interested in buying, HP asks you to provide a name and email address, to which they'll send you more information.

And, just like that, HP has a lead.

The Difference Between Search vs. Display Network

With the Nissan ad, Google's Search Network reaches people who actively look for a certain keyword, or something very close to it.

The HP technology ad, on the other hand, was an example of Google's Display Network at play. The Network is made up of thousands of sites who've all agreed to host advertising from other companies.

That's it.

Advantages of Google Advertising

With Google's search-based ads, they provide the best quality leads. The prospect doesn't have to be tricked, entertained, or gently seduced into making a purchase - they've actively looked up the product or service and stated their interest. This is very good news for companies who are solution and results oriented.

Likewise, with Google's Display Network, campaigns have far more reach than they ever could on Facebook. The display network consists of over a million news sites, blogs, articles, and other websites that accept text ads, banner ads and video ads from Google AdWords. A huge channel is YouTube, the second biggest search engine on the internet. On YouTube, you can create pre-roll videos and show ads to people who've already searched for a product on another search engine. Obviously, this benefit is extremely valuable.

And, with Google AdWords, once you've mastered optimisation, you can happily produce steady results for months or even years. This is a huge benefit over Facebook, which bends you over backwards with constant demands for more content and creativity.

The Disadvantages of Google Advertising

It's very competitive, tricky to use, and the results are rarely instantaneous.

When AdWords was brand new, there were lots of inexpensive clicks to be had, and people could get away with lots of little, cheap mistakes.

That's not the case any longer. Certain keywords have upped in value due to demand, and a cost per click can be anything up to $30, depending on the time of day and the competition. In an effort to keep up, some marketers have set a ridiculously high daily budget, then panicked when they've received a $3,000 bill they've got no idea how to pay for.

AdWords optimisation takes a long time to perfect, and many advertisers have to go through a long trial-and-error period before things fall into place. AdWord's menus and instructions can also be slightly misleading, meaning marketers have made some hugely expensive mistakes before they've realised there's anything wrong.

For that reason, I'm not going to recommend a search-based campaign within this book. The idea is to make money, not put you out of pocket.

For your particular needs, the best way to use Google AdWords would be with a brand campaign.

Google AdWords Brand Campaign

According to Google:

"The purpose of a brand-engagement campaign is to build awareness of and positive associations with your company and its products and services. A customer can interact with your brand in a variety of ways, including watching videos, playing games, spending time on your website, or communicating with other customers."

Brand Campaigns include your brand's name as a keyword and any possible misspellings.

A Brand Campaign can help you:

- Increase interactions with your brand
- Build positive brand associations
- Increase brand loyalty by connecting with your target audience
- Motivate customers to engage with your brand and, therefore, your product or service

Let me give you a real-life example.

We are currently running Facebook and Google AdWord campaigns for Aunt Meg, a debt advice service targeted specifically at struggling or single mothers. Unfortunately, words like "debt consolidation" are hugely valuable on Google, and the cost per click would be higher than our budget would allow.

So, instead of pouring money into expensive phrases such as "debt help" or "credit card debt consolidation", we spent it on the words "Aunt Meg". We knew that if we bid on "Aunt Meg" there would be zero competition and we'd only pay a few pennies per click.

This tactic also coincided nicely with our social media campaign on Facebook. A customer would see the ad and wonder if the company was legitimate. A quick Google search would confirm this and, as a result, the prospect would be far more likely to engage with the service.

It's Important To Get In There Quickly

Brand names of Google AdWords aren't off-limits when it comes to bidding. If you're not bidding on your company name, someone else may take advantage of that opportunity and will show up in the search engine BEFORE you. With enough competitors bidding on your ad name, it's possible you'll lose valuable clicks. If you're a business owner, you should always check. Type in your brand name and see if one of your competitors is being cheeky.

Controlling the Message

Another benefit of bidding on your brand name is controlling the message. Creating new ad copy for your brand campaign will let you test different messages in your ad, and measure their performance. These tests could help you decide whether you should update your organic listing text.

For example, in a paid ad campaign you could include a call-to-action, or a special offer that won't appear in your organic listing. Even if you don't have any competition for the name of your brand, taking advantage and advertising bonuses is a brilliant way to pull in more customers.

You can also link your paid ads to multiple landing pages, depending on the offers you displayed in each. If, for Aunt Meg, I offered a free consultation, the link I provided could take you straight to the sign-up on the landing page.

Brand Performance

According to Search Engine Land, studies show that paid ads convert better than organic listings by up to 32%. Surveys also show that customers have a better brand recall when a company ran a paid advertisement alongside organic. If you want to ensure your brand sticks in the mind of your prospect, make sure your organic and paid searches work well enough together to give your brand authenticity. Remember that branding goes well beyond just a logo or some fancy graphics. Use your adverts, landing pages and funnels to create an entire customer experience that's instantly recognisable.

Chapter 2

Why Marketing Agencies (Or In-House Marketing Teams) Are Failing You

Why Expensive Marketing Agencies Often Don't Deliver

Lead generation is vital for most businesses. Depending on your product or service, the amount needed may vary - some will need hundreds of leads a day, others only two big sales a year. The fact of the matter is, leads are the lifeblood of any company, and it's impossible to survive without a steady stream of qualified enquiries.

With business hours the way they are, it can be daunting to get through all the priorities of the day without worrying about generating leads. One way to get past this, and employed by thousands of small to medium companies, is to hire a marketing agency and leave it in their hands.

I get it. Having a whole team of people taking care of your brand seems really tempting, especially as it gives you the chance to focus your attention elsewhere. But is it a luxury you can afford?

Have you paid thousands to an agency and been left disappointed with the results? Marketing agencies charge a hefty fee for their services, and their results are often less than overwhelming. It's like starting the day with a pocketful of coins, then coming home for dinner suspiciously lighter with a gaping tear where the money should be.

What I've learned is: if you want something done correctly, you need to do it yourself.

Before you sign any dotted lines, remember that a marketing agency is also a business. This means it has all the things to deal with that you do, like taxes, salaries and expenses. To cover these, most marketing agencies will ask you for a retainer fee, a three-month contract, and a minimum spend before they'll even try and get you one lead. It's a tough call for any business to make without seeing any results, but some companies are so desperate they'll agree to anything to make things work.

A lot of people say the one con of having a retainer contract is, on certain months, it may be a struggle to find enough work to send the agency. This could potentially lead to unused retainer time and a lot of wasted money. An agency should have a realistic understanding of how much time your company needs, and be ready to apply feedback to use their and your time as effectively as possible.

Unfortunately, a lot of marketing agencies won't actually provide the feedback and analysis needed. Once they've had the retainer, an agency is very unlikely to pull out all the stops for you, as they're working on a flat-fee. Say, for example, the agency is generating your company 100 leads a month. You're reasonably happy with this, but think 200 or 300 would be better. How would you achieve this? By giving the marketing agency more money.

No business is going to work double or triple as hard without a hefty profit to show for it.

Another con: while you're focused solely on your business, your marketing agency has a lot of different clients. When you first start with an agency, you can expect to be showered with attention. They'll share with you every detail, hold weekly calls with you to keep track of their progress and, for a short time, everything will run like clockwork.

Until the next client comes along.

Recent studies show that SEO specialists in large marketing agencies can handle as many as 17 separate accounts. Once another client is added to the mix, offering more money than you ever could, you can only watch from the sidelines as they enjoy more attention and higher priority status. This can even lead to your deadlines being pushed further and further back - a nightmare for anyone on a tight budget and with floundering sales.

On top of the retainer fee, a marketing agency will charge for all the extras. So, if you wanted them to redesign your website, shoot some videos or write content, they would charge you for these services with a huge markup. As I've explained in previous sections, with the age of digital now at its peak, these services have become cheaper, not more expensive. A marketing agency, on the other hand, has a "you can't do it without us" attitude. This means they can charge as much as they want, and struggling companies will agree to pay because they don't have time to learn how to do it themselves.

With a few hours of learning and a bit of time for preparation, all of these things can be done **entirely in-house**. As I've mentioned before, online firms like Unbounce make the building of beautiful, professional sites a "drag and drop" experience. Starting from as little as $79 per month, with WordPress, HubSpot and Infusionsoft integrations, plus 125 templates to choose from, choosing to buy should be a no-brainer. Most marketing agencies start at $2000 a month, *without* extras.

As for videos, I've been shooting my own for years. After I invested in my own camera and lighting equipment, which cost me a few thousand dollars, I began to rent a local studio for as little as a few hundred dollars per shoot. Recently, I managed to rent out the office next door to our own. It's perfect for video shoots, and we're working hard to make it into our personal studio.

Inspired by Unbounce, I started creating a few script templates and tested them all in front of an audience. The ones that worked best I still use today, only tweaking as required. All these scripts are working as well as ever and still bring in the leads I need. After my initial investment and hard work, getting a script together is free - not the $1000 a pop to hire a freelance copywriter.

I've also found you need to be careful of very expensive freelancers or agencies whose main selling point is X number of years in the field. In the marketing world, longer doesn't necessarily mean better. Chances are, these people spent years honing their craft when PPC and lead generation was still new, back in 1997 or the early millennium, and they've been playing catch-up ever since. In the boom of the digital age, marketing can turn on its head in as little as 6 months, with new strategies, new platforms and brand new fads. These people may be able to talk a good game and charge a lot of money, but if they're sticking rigidly to old, dinosaur strategies, this could damage your business in the long run. You haven't got the time to be left behind - you need to be constantly learning, developing and exploring the unknown.

It's Not An Agency, It's My Own Marketing Team!

If you've worked hard enough to have your own marketing team, you must be well aware of how frustrating it is when they're not performing up to demand.

The truth is, lots of in-house marketing teams fail for the same reason the agencies do. It's because they're being paid a flat salary and, no matter how hard they work, that fee isn't going to change. Long hours and little rewards will turn even the most hardworking employees into average players, skimming along the ice and doing just enough to keep themselves upright. The ones that *do* constantly push forward, learn, evolve and experiment will stay in an in-house agency long enough to cut their teeth in the industry and learn the basics. Then they'll leave and go elsewhere, charging lots of money for all the things they've learned from *your* business.

There are four warning signs that your marketing team needs help.

- Reluctance to try and test new ideas and advertising platforms.
- Inconsistent lead volume and rising "cost per lead".
- Simple ideas taking forever to implement. For example, a new landing page that takes months to perfect and go live. They'll blame IT, but lack of adhering to deadlines is always a slippery slope.
- The team expects and relies on outside help. They are more focused on employing and managing agencies than doing it for themselves.

If this sounds like your marketing team, take a seat for a moment and breathe. The next section of this book will tell you how to avoid further mistakes with marketing agencies, and how to give your in-house team a much-needed boost.

Everyone on my team is self-taught, including myself. There's never been a better time to learn, grow, and build an asset for the business. Chapter 3 will help you through the hiring process, to fill out any gaps you may have in your current marketing department.

Chapters 4 and 5 will provide you and your team with all the technical know-how on how to create your Facebook campaigns, use Unbounce and get those leads pouring in faster than water through an open dam.

If They Can't Do It, How Can I?

The good news about digital marketing is it's still relatively new. There's no degree to be explicitly earned in Facebook advertising and Google AdWords; no four years snoozing your way through lectures or a $60,000+ debt to pay off.

On the other hand, there's no stopping anyone from taking a two-day, $97 course, then promoting themselves as a professional.

These courses are often run by self-proclaimed "gurus", who promise to teach you all about digital marketing in the space of a couple of hours and a two-sided A4 pamphlet. Largely, these workshops spend about 75% of the time flattering the crowd ("anyone can do it! If you're as smart as I know you are, you'll see it's a walk in the park!"), 15% of the time actually sharing some basic "facts", and the last 10% trying to sell tickets to another talk or seminar. Audiences walk out feeling enlightened and good about themselves. They try something at home and, down to beginner's luck or whatever you want to call it, they get a few results.

But you wouldn't watch an episode of David Attenborough's *Blue Planet* and tell everyone you're a qualified Marine Biologist.

Unfortunately, these fake gurus are everywhere, and they can be disastrous for a small or medium business trying to find their feet. Soaring on the wings of their first, lucky, success, these "gurus" will charge you an extortionate fee for services, then cut you loose when the going gets tough.

If you come across any of these gurus, I suppose the best thing to do would be to listen to what they have to say and make notes.

And then you need to do the exact opposite.

Being good at anything isn't easy. It's not something you learn in a day, or a month, or even a year. It takes hard work and silly mistakes, heaped with all the peaks and troughs that come with trying to get better at what you do.

I made the same mistakes when I was starting out. I signed up for a few newsletters and read a few stories. The next thing I knew, I was marketing myself as an SEO professional. For a while, everything was going well.

Then, I lost everything.

My SEO techniques killed my clients' rankings, and my business partner ran out on me, taking our seven local business clients with him.

Thankfully, when the going got tough, my parents had taught me the value of responsibility. I shouldered my mistakes and swore I'd learn from them. It took me six years to master the art of lead generation and I'm still learning new things every day.

And that's what taking your marketing out of the hands of an agency and into your own in-house department is about: responsibility. If you build and manage your own campaigns, you take accountability for your mistakes, alterations, data and successes. You'll be able to spot the problems immediately and won't be dependent on a third-party.

Because an agency won't tell you when they get things wrong. They'll agree to your terms and ask for a big fat fee to cover their services. If you're a small or medium business, they'll probably put your campaigns in the hands of a junior member of staff who won't have accumulated the skills to get the results you want. And, because they're frightened of being fired, or looking unprofessional, it'll take them right up to the deadline to admit they haven't got the clout to carry it through.

A marketing agency is built on the concept of illusion and, when that illusion shatters, things can get ugly. Unless they're willing to sit down with you and talk over the brief, an agency will usually vomit a load of half-formed facts and lazy data at you, and hope you'll be swept along for the ride. They'll try to persuade you to pay them for impressions (a simple view or click on your ad), rather than conversions (a qualified prospect). When it comes to the details, like the copy, funnels or how a landing page converts, most agencies don't have the time, skill or staff to fix it for you. As you can imagine, this will stop a campaign dead in its tracks.

According to emarketer.com, 44% of businesses are now looking to form their own in-house ad team. Statistics also say:

- 86% of SMBs are looking for increased speed and agility within their in-house marketing teams
- 68% are looking for improved cost efficiencies

- 54% want the operational control that comes with working in the same building
- 61% want better brand expertise
- 52% are looking for enhanced collaboration between teams

If you're a business who's got their own in-house marketing team and still aren't getting the right results, ask yourself the following questions:

- Do you feel like you have operational control over your campaigns?
- Are your team meeting all their deadlines and communicating as they should be?
- Crucially, are your advertisements attracting leads?

If the answer to all these questions is a slightly deflated "no", then you need to keep reading and act before these problems damage your business' growth.

You've got a couple of quick fixes at hand before you need to do anything drastic.

When it comes to deadlines, for example, you could try repurposing old successful content, instead of creating new posts. All you need to do is alter the format, use a new image, and change a couple of lines. If your original post garnered successful feedback, reintroducing the information could get you the same attention again. You also may catch a few new customers who haven't seen the ad before.

For other things, like operational control and communication, you can ensure your in-house team are measuring the metrics that matter. So, instead of keeping track of website traffic, you could supervise your cost per lead for some ads, and see which are the most effective. In turn, you could run an analysis of how well your landing page converts, and ask your team to report back.

However, these are usually only temporary fixes, and you could still see yourself running into problems. In this case, your marketing team is in need of longer-term support.

To get to my point: it may be time to consider appointing new staff, such as a graduate with the technical know-how, to do what you want. Sometimes, recurring problems can be fixed with new talent to plug the skill gaps.

With eight of my own employees, hiring is something that I'm used to. I'll tell you all my top tips and talk you through my hiring funnel in the next chapter.

Chapter 3

Expanding Your Marketing Team Efficiently

How Many People Do I Need To Make This Work?

In 1624, as he recovered from a severe but unknown sickness, the poet John Donne penned this line: "No man is an island entire of itself".

Convinced he was dying of multiple illnesses, Donne composed *Devotions upon Emergent Occasions*, a 23-part prose work that described each step of his sickness, day-by-day, as he reflected on the concept of internal sin manifesting itself as disease. To this day, "no man is an island" is a popular idiom in the Western world, uttered as a warning to those who try to accomplish anything significant on their own.

Personally, I find this phrase a bit of a downer.

The main difference between you, the reader, and John Donne is you're not dying. On the contrary, you're trying every way possible to build and develop a thriving B2C business, with high-quality leads pumping through its veins.

Everything I explain in this book can be done, and done effectively, by one person: you. In fact, I recommend you implement what I'm teaching in this book on your own. Make yourself an island, get to the point where you're comfortable doing everything within these pages. Teach yourself to lead by example and know what you do inside out. That's the first step toward marketing mastery.

By bringing your lead generation in-house, *you're* the one with the high intellectual capacity, the entrepreneurial spirit, and the ability to lead and manage your own ideas.

Once you're confident with the material, it may be time to start levelling up. As a business takes on more work and nets more successes, expansion is a natural part of its life-cycle. For this reason, it's worth thinking about what resources you have and what you will need in the future.

You, for example, may currently be a marketing team of one. This means you're looking after all three phases of the process:

- Traffic generation
- Soft conversion (a lead)
- Hard conversion (a sale)

This could be working very well for you, for now. My templates in Chapters 4 and 5 will help you create perfect campaigns, landing pages and advertorials, and enough of them to do the job. But, as an expanding business, you may find it easier to start separating these phases and allocating them to other people.

In a team of just three, one person could generate and create all the content, another could work on content distribution, and the final hire could focus on managing all the social networking accounts.

Naturally, with less of a burden on one person, the quality of work will rise. Good quality work means better leads, and better leads mean a higher ROI.

You'll see in the contents page I've included 5 Reasons To Hire a Graduate later on in this book. For a newly-expanding marketing team, a graduate's a perfect choice. In most cases, FlexxDigital starts a graduate's salary on $22,000, and it will rise from there significantly if he or she delivers. We've found this to be a fairly competitive wage, and got some good, bright hires for this kind of money. For an agency's basic services, you'll be looking at around $2000 - $3000 a month.

If you make the commitment to expanding your in-house team now, it'll save a lot of headaches, wasted time and money. With a set of employees, you'll be in control of what goes in and out of the company and when. You'll certainly be at the top of your own priority list.

But, what if you don't want to build a team from scratch? You're a medium to large business, have a marketing team, and want to make your existing one perform better.

Hand on heart, I have never met any business that performs to the level my company does. Usually, this isn't down to lack of hard work or effort, but because they haven't been educating themselves and moving with the times. Fortunately for you, the lessons in this book can be used to retrain underperforming teams.

The tools I'm sharing with you are very easy to use. There is no coding experience or web development knowledge required. If you have someone in your marketing team who has the right mindset, can problem solve, and gets things done, you'll be absolutely fine.

First, you'll need someone who wants to write great ads. This book will teach you how, and we'll give you access to a swipe file containing templates for hard-hitting headlines and copy.

You'll also need an enthusiastic creative who wants to learn how to write advertorials and pre-sales letters. I will give you examples of what's worked for us in the health insurance industry, and you'll be able to download these via a link. In Chapter 5, I'll share my notes on how to craft advertorials and landing pages, which you can share as a free resource with members of your in-house marketing team. These notes and templates have helped me generate millions of clicks, which have led to millions of dollars worth of income. I will show you how to upload the models onto Unbounce and tweak them to suit your own needs.

Again, there are **no web design skills needed** here. The final stage of building a successful campaign is to understand Facebook and Google advertising platforms, which I have detailed in Chapter 4.

From now, the only thing holding you back is your own self-doubt. Some people, those with a decade or more of marketing experience, may be resistant to implementing new ideas or strategies. This kind of attitude can become a problem, as it will erode the mindset of the whole team. In this case, you can think about assigning different tasks or a new position to the person in question. If this is impossible, or they're unwilling, you need to let them go.

For optimal success, you need to determine the will, skills and knowledge of every existing member of your marketing team. If, for example, you have a smart and passionate employee with some gaps in their knowledge, that's not a huge problem. Pair them for a couple of weeks with someone you know has the experience, and they'll soon catch up.

However, anyone with a bad attitude, or who is unwilling to learn, is not going to do well for your company. As you sit and wait for improvement, precious leads are slipping through your fingers. Try a warning and, if there's no improvement, it's time to say goodbye. It doesn't make you Machiavelli. It ensures everyone is finally on the same page.

5 Reasons To Hire A Graduate

Sometimes you can fix significant or recurring problems within your in-house marketing team by hiring someone who can plug the skill gaps.

Hiring can be a strangely evocative word. It's one that can induce anything from a mild cold sweat to a razor-slice of panic right in the guts.

It's not a process that thrills most employers, even when the work's piled ceiling high and the office's only feature wall consists of about 1000 Post-It notes dating as far back as 2001. Hiring is usually tiring, time-consuming and expensive.

Which makes it all the more urgent you choose the right candidate for the job. According to a study by LeadershipIQ, "46% of newly-hired employees will fail in the first 18 months, while only 19% will achieve unequivocal success."

Surprisingly, it's not their technical abilities that lead these new hires towards failure, but their poor interpersonal skills. The study found that 26% of new hires fail because they refuse to accept feedback, 23% because they can't manage their emotions, 17% lack the motivation to excel, and 15% because they have the wrong temperament for the job.

Only 11% are fired or quit because they lack the necessary technical skills.

Having a new employee get up and leave within 18 months can be a pain for any business. According to a 2007 report in *Training* magazine, companies spend an average of $1,200 a year training one employee (with inflation as it is, that's about $1,500 now). Add on the cost of recruitment (about $7,645 according to National Association of Colleges and Employers), and the worker's salary (say, $24,000 minimum), and you're looking at a total hire cost of $33,145 for the first year alone.

Can you afford to spend that, and more, every 18 months?

Admittedly, the idea of hiring a graduate is even more contentious. With 40% of UK adults possessing one degree or more, a university qualification is no longer a sign of quality.

And, according to the BBC website, businesses say they aren't finding enough savvy graduates who can start contributing from day one on the job. Fundamentally, recent graduates think they have more work-based skills than they actually do. According to CareerBuilder, surveyed employers believe many UK graduates are lacking in essential qualities such as problem-solving (60%), creative thinking (56%), and interpersonal skills (50%). Even internships are no longer the mark of a great candidate: many employers think applicants embellish their experience and spend a lot more time making coffee and fetching sandwiches than they'd like to admit.

If this sounds like you're sinking into some sort of nightmare, I have some good news.

For all the reasons not to hire a graduate, there are about 10 more reasons why you should. I'm not going to waste time listing them all, so here's five to get you started:

1. **They're affordable.** Most of you picked up this book because you wanted to know how to generate hundreds of leads in-house, every day, and see your business' profits skyrocket. This isn't going to happen if you hire someone with 30+ years in the field. With age comes experience and experience comes at a cost. A graduate, on the other hand, isn't expecting a six-figure salary in their first job. With few professional skills early on, a graduate will be happy to settle for lower pay in exchange for experience and training.

2. **Speed to value.** Unlike the rest of us, where Facebook and AdWords are still relatively new, graduates are more tech-savvy. Having grown-up and evolved in an automated age, they have a natural aptitude for new technologies and the ever-changing digital landscape. Fresh out of university, graduates know all the latest industry principles, business models and success stories. They've also put in the time and energy into staying up-to-date with current fields – which saves *you* time and money in training and professional development.

3. **They're a blank canvas.** Your rules are the first rules a graduate's going to learn in the workplace. You have the opportunity to shape them into what you need, so they become part of the company's culture. Graduates have also developed a habit of learning, so will seek to acquire more knowledge in the workplace.

4. **Succession planning.** Take on a graduate and provide them with a career path. If you build the road for them to get to a management level, you'll also solve any future succession planning concerns. And if you make it clear their career path holds opportunity for progression, it'll give them more incentive not to leave.

5. **They may be smarter than you.** Lee Iacocca, the American automobile executive best-known for pioneering the development of the Ford Mustang and Pinto Cars, said this about hiring: "I hire the people brighter than me, and I get out of their way."

   To make something clear, I'm not saying that going to university makes you a genius. There have been plenty of talented people who skipped higher education and carved out wonderful careers. If you meet that kind of person, that's more than fine. Hire them on the spot. In all probability, they were lucky enough to find their niche at an early age and have the discipline to self-teach.

   But, in an age where one job advertisement in the UK can attract as many as 250 CVs, sorting the wheat from the chaff can be trying - especially when you have a million other things to do.

   Finding a graduate with the right kinds of skills could be one of the best ways to boost your company. Once they've had some proper training, and you've assessed their personality (more on this later), you should be able to leave the building, running, and analysis of campaigns in their capable hands. If you put yourself in the position of coordinator, your hire will know you care about and trust them. In turn, the goodwill from both ends will translate into good work.

How To Write A Job Description

Writing is a form of communicating, and the latter is a fundamental human skill. Unfortunately, whether it be written or verbal, some people can't communicate well.

A job description is *your* chance to communicate. Fitting together the perfect job ad is actually a bit of a puzzle. You need to be able to encourage suitable candidates to join the company without whitewashing the details of the job involved. It's also your first opportunity to screen incoming applicants.

For example, you could ask all candidates to email their application with a specific subject line and in a PDF format. You'll be surprised (or not) by how many people mess this up by missing it off completely. Though it's a finicky detail, and can be frustrating for those who've spent a couple of hours tailoring their cover letter, you have to be tough. You need someone capable of following instructions right off the bat. You'll also be teaching the candidate a valuable lesson - I guarantee they'll read all the details in their next job application.

For the job description itself, make sure you include all the following points:

- **An appealing job title.** Even if the actual job is nothing to get too excited about, a good title with strong keywords will attract the kind of candidates you're looking for.

- **A short introduction.** This shouldn't be more than a few lines and should talk more about the job than the company at this point. It's okay to say, "We're so great, come and work for us!" but if the job seeker has no idea what the position entails they'll just move on.

- **List 3 to 7 main responsibilities.** No list is exhaustive, and most people will find themselves doing crazy stuff in the name of work at 4pm on a Thursday afternoon. But, remember, this advert isn't a job description. Post enough of the role's main elements to ensure the right candidates send in their CVs.

- **Mention your location.** Do you want to hire candidates across the UK or would you rather they were local? If you mention this in the job ad, potential candidates will take their time to research the town, transport links, and whether they can or want to move. Putting in something like location can dramatically cut the number of applications. This may sound like a bad thing but, on the flipside, it reduces the number of candidates turning down an interview because they were hit with a 200-mile travel distance.

- **List the salary.** Even a ballpark figure is helpful, here. If the wage depends on experience, give your minimum and maximum figures - e.g. $20,000 - $27,000. A job's salary is also a good indicator of the level of expertise and responsibility expected in the role. It's worth noting that some job seekers will be suspicious of vacancies without a listed salary. It signals that the company doesn't know how much they're willing to pay, or the wage will be lower than average for the role it's advertising, or the employer is holding out to see if they can pay less than they expected.

- **Write about your company.** Unless your business is as big as McDonald's or what you do is in the company name, your potential applicants will need to know what industry you're in. A couple of paragraphs should suffice, and try to relate the description to the role. If the job seeker wants to know more, they'll do their own research and look up your site.

- **Make sure spelling and grammar are correct.** You expect your applicants to have a firm grasp of spelling and grammar, and you should lead by example. I've seen my fair share of job ads littered with mistakes, formatting errors and, once, even an invalid email address. A rushed job ad will discredit your company and drive away your more serious candidates.

Hiring intelligently is one of the best ways to build a company's success. Some managers don't want to be outshone by the creativity, skills and experience of a new employee. You, on the other hand, welcome new ideas, new methods and inventive uses of technology - anything to ramp up those lead numbers and send your profits through the roof.

The Test Tasks

Test tasks have worked exceptionally well for us in the digital marketing space, and they're what I refer to as my "hiring funnel". Strictly speaking, the tasks can come before or after an interview - it's up to you. Some employers prefer to interview first, then set the task to see if the applicant's work is as good as their talk. Others prefer to send the task first, then only interview the best candidates for the job. Either way works.

I prefer to set the test tasks before I offer anyone an interview. This way, I've already leafed through the 250 CVs and found 12-20 I've really liked. Depending on how well they've done on the assignments (immediately discounting those who've not included the specific subject line in their email, or who have failed to put their work into a PDF format), I should be left with about 6-10 people I want to interview. I've seen how they work, I've looked at their strengths, and - especially if it was a writing task- they've subconsciously given me some precious insight into their personality.

As we mentioned before, an employer faces many challenges when it comes to making the right decision. In an interview, buzzwords like "good team player", "detail-oriented", and "extensive experience" hang so thick in the air, it's hard to see the real candidate behind the smog of jargon. An applicant is there to prove themselves to you, with the sole goal of securing the job. With so much at stake, some candidates will lie, while others will be crippled by nerves. Without a test task, it's easy for an interviewer to hire the best *politician* rather than the best person for the role.

Fortunately, an assignment is a quick, easy and cheap way to see if a candidate's skills match their experience. If you supply the task before offering an interview, it also helps to weed out applicants who are A) all talk, B) not actually interested in the job, or C) not quite ready for the role you're offering.

Before I show you an example of a test task I use in my own company, here are a few things to keep in mind when setting assignments.

1. **Ask candidates to email their work with a specific subject line and in PDF format**. As mentioned earlier, you need to reduce the possible candidates down to those who can follow instructions. Think of these less as "traps" and more of a necessary route towards eliminating candidates from a swollen, boggy interview process.

2. **Set a concrete deadline**. If you're sending the tasks via email, give them a couple of hours to open the message

first. Depending on how long you think the assignment will take, allow the applicant anywhere between 48 hours to 7 days. If they miss the deadline, they're out of the running.

3. **Be precise and make the task simple**. One way to guarantee a whole host of bad applications is to communicate what you're after poorly. If you want something summed-up in less than a paragraph, say so. If you're looking at a longer piece of writing, note the key points you want to appear. A nervous or enthusiastic candidate is much more likely to overwrite than underwrite and could spend 10 hours polishing a 7-page article you'll then need to read.

If a candidate wants the job you're offering, they won't shy away from doing a test task - and if they do, you know not to hire them. Anyone can say they "think outside the box", but the assignment gives them the chance to prove they're up to the job. If they've done their research and thought about the task properly, turning in a quality piece of work can be just the thing to distinguish themselves from other candidates. It goes without saying that these are the people you want to hire.

To get you started, here's an example of a job specification and test task below. I recently used this one to hire my PPC Manager.

PPC Manager (The "Rockstar Role): The Job Description

We are an online lead generation agency who delivers web leads via PPC advertising.

We specialise in lead generation through Adwords, Facebook, Twitter. Taboola, Outbrain and more.
https://www.screencast.com/t/OQ3p2he7

DESCRIPTION:
A great ground floor opportunity to join a relatively young lead generation agency based in central Hove as an Adwords Manager.

We're a small team with a big mission - to be the absolute most talented, cutting-edge lead generation digital marketing agency in the UK.

Are you an experienced AdWords Ninja? Do you want to manage £1m+ per annum of PPC spend via our lead generation websites? Do you want free reign to test new strategies without having to deal with a 'client' or a 'marketing manager'?

If so, Flexx is the place to be. We have a few traditional 'clients' but the bulk of our business is lead gen via websites we have built in-house.

It means that you will have access to significant budgets to test test test! We also do a lot of native advertising, so if you haven't had much experience with that then you will learn plenty!

Are you up for that?

PREREQUISITES INCLUDE:

1. Data Analysis – finding 'stories' in data from Google Analytics and advertising platforms

2. Using Microsoft excel to communicate those 'stories'

3. Manage paid advertising campaigns, mainly Google Adwords:

- Manage and perform daily account responsibilities associated with Google AdWords, Yahoo, Bing and other search platforms for a variety of clients.
- Maintain and monitor keyword bids, account daily and monthly budget caps, impression share, quality score and other important account metrics.
- Manage large keyword lists.
- Provide creative copy suggestions and graphical ad templates.
- Manage Display network placement lists on AdWords and through other contextual advertising platforms.
- Provide recommendations and execute strategies for keyword opportunities, campaign structuring, targeting, display network, and other facets of paid search in accordance with client goals.
- Generate new paid search campaigns, ad groups, and accounts and aid in the creation of new paid search marketing initiatives.
- Generate weekly and monthly client reporting for all major metrics, goals tracking, revenue tracking, and other paid search initiatives.
- Keep pace with search engine and PPC industry trends and developments.
- Monitor and administer web analytics dashboards, reports and key reporting tools, and point out key areas of importance in accordance client goals.
- Monitor and evaluate search results and search performance across the major search channels.
- Communication to team and management on project development, timelines, and results.

- Work closely with the other team members to meet client goals.

Pretty cool right?

We also use a lot of automation in our business - you will, therefore, be working heavily with a platform called PPC Samurai to build scripts and automation.

If you love numbers, if you love strategy, if you are just a tiny bit 'geeky' then you will LOVE working for us.

SKILLS:

A great attitude, a willingness to learn, and the ability to move fast.

You will need intermediate to expert experience, but you will also be trained on the job.

If you know your way around a bit of code, even better.

HOW TO APPLY:

You will not be granted an interview until you have completed this task:

http://flexxdigital.com/adwords-rockstar-position/

We will be in touch after that.

PPC Manager (The "Rockstar Role): The Test Task

Thank you for taking interest in the PPC Rockstar Role.

At Flexx Digital, we find resumes don't really give us the whole picture of your ability and skills.

That's why we have created a two-part task for all our applicants which will demonstrate their skills.

Please read the instructions carefully and complete the task below.

TASK:

We have compiled the results of a real paid traffic campaign. You can see those results here [link to the results].

As a digital agency, we regularly have to display our results to our clients in ways they can easily understand. So, first, we'd like you to make charts clearly showing each of the following:

1. A chart showing the amount of leads according to age group
2. A chart showing the amount of leads according to gender
3. A chart showing the amount of leads according to impression device

Secondly, in our paid traffic campaigns we are always looking to provide the highest volume of leads at the lowest possible cost. To get the best results we need to show our adverts to the best possible audience.

We'd like you to create a customer avatar that shows us a member of our ideal target audience. Use the example results above to inform your avatar.

You can access the customer avatar template here [add link].

Finally, send your charts and your customer avatar in PDF format, along with your resume, to dan@flexxdigital.com with subject line "PPC Rockstar".

We'd love to see how you approach this task. Good luck!

***

As an added bonus and comparison, I've also included the test task for a videographer - a very sought after position, both for employers and employees. Our advertisement on Wired Sussex proved to be extremely popular, with over 200 applicants. With this test task, we managed to narrow down the candidates to six suitable for interview.

Videographer: The Test Task

Film, edit, export and send us a 20 - 30-second video that would be a suitable advertisement for Facebook. See some examples of ads towards the end of these instructions.

CONTENT:
The video should show 3 different ways to do something. Feel free to use a friend as your subject while you shoot. As long as it's filmed and edited by you, we don't mind!

Here are some ideas to get you started:
3 ways to make a sandwich
3 ways to tie your shoes
3 ways to make a paper aeroplane

REQUIREMENTS:

Create or find any logo to use in a transitional intro section of the video.

Video record 3 different ways to do 'something.'

Regarding audio, we'd love to see if you could explain these '3 ways' (and perhaps drop in some royalty free music too), then add some subtitles in post-production.

Add a 'call-to-action' button in the video outro, letting viewers know to subscribe, buy or download some content of your choosing. This is obviously fake, we just need to see it within the video.

Create a thumbnail or take a video still and export as a png with a resolution of 1200px by 628px.

Export the video file as .mp4 and email with the video thumbnail to [your email].

FACEBOOK VIDEO AD EXAMPLES:
3 Ways To Make Bacon
3 Creative Coffee Hacks
DIY Curtain Tiebacks, 3 Ways

***

As you can see, this task leaves plenty of room for creativity, as well as clear instructions for what's we expect from the candidate. If the applicant is worth their salt, they'll take the ideas and run with them. Again, it's entirely up to you whether you want to set these tasks before or after the interview.

Which leads me to the next section in Chapter 3: Interviewing and Making A Decision.

Interviewing and Making A Decision

How to interview is a skill I've learned through plenty of experience and lots of hard lessons. If you get hiring wrong, it can set you back six months to a year. It's worth hiring slowly and taking your time. I'm getting better and better at it, but it's definitely still a work in progress.

With the art of interviewing so difficult to master, it's a good idea to layer your process. I tend to tier my interviews into three distinct stages: a phone interview, a face-to-face meeting then, finally, a Kolbe personality test. Though this method can feel like you're wading knee-deep through mud, it helps ensure the candidate you choose meets your company's standards, along with possessing the talent and mindset that will contribute to your growth.

The Telephone Interview

The telephone interview is designed to be quick and gets the "standard" questions out of the way before I ask the meatier ones in the face-to-face interview. Any applicant worth their salt should be well used to these types of inquiries, and should be able to answer them readily, thoroughly and well. To help me out (as I can telephone up to 15 candidates for one role), I utilise a quick "scoring" template for each candidate, marking their answers from 1 (poor) to 5 (excellent). The criteria I'm looking for are communication skills, energy, intelligence, logic, and work ethic. You can mark these areas independently, but I tend to take all factors into account and give one mark per question.

1. Why did you leave your current role? /5
2. What can you offer in this role that somebody else cannot? /5
3. What are three things your former manager would like you to improve on?/5
4. Name a time you made a mistake. Tell me how you handled it. /5
5. What is one of your most significant accomplishments? How did it affect your career, and what barriers did you need to overcome? /5
6. Tell me about a time you went above and beyond the requirements for a project./5
7. What do you expect from a manager? /5
8. What type of company environment most contributes to your success? /5

Once I've gone through the telephone interview results, I'm usually left with about five or six people I want to meet face-to-face. Even if you're lucky enough to have interviewed 10 high-scorers, try and narrow down your decisions as much as you can. You'll be saving yourself a lot of time and money in the long-run.

The beauty of doing the telephone interview first means I can ask some more interesting, detailed questions in the direct conversation. At this point, I already have a lot of information about my candidates; I know they work well, thanks to the test task, and I know they've got great telephone skills thanks to the phone interview.

The Face-To-Face Interview

A face-to-face meeting is a different state of affairs. A telephone interview is far less pressure on a candidate (provided they have excellent telephone skills), as they're in a familiar environment, their own clothes, and probably have some form of notes in front of them. When you're first introduced to your interviewees, keep an eye out for the following qualities:

1. Punctuality
2. State of dress
3. Articulation
4. Confidence
5. Good energy
6. Cognitive skills
7. The questions they ask
8. Whether they'd be a good fit

Every applicant knows they need to make an excellent first impression. However, not everybody knows a first impression is locked in within seven seconds of meeting. These seven seconds are crucial for you, unfair as it may seem, as you don't have a lot of time. If a candidate sounded confident on the phone, then can't make eye contact when you're in the room, you know they struggle with or withdraw from immediate social pressure.

When it comes to interview questions, play as safe, or go as wild, as you like. You could consider using original questions if you'd think it would help fill the position. Microsoft started using these questions in the 1990s to measure a candidate's mental flexibility, entrepreneurial potential and imagination. Since then, other top companies such as Google, Facebook and Amazon have started integrating them into the hiring process. In case you're unaware of the hype, here are a few examples:

"Why are manhole covers round?" - Google

"If you were a pizza delivery man, how would you benefit from scissors?" - Apple

"How would you describe the colour yellow to a blind person?"
- Spirit Airlines

Chances are, these questions would be the last thing a candidate expects, and you'll be able to see them use their problem-solving skills in a pressurised environment - just like at work. Be warned, though: businesses don't really need the type of people who can answer these in an abstract way. This type of interview technique could backfire and alienate the applicant, driving them to turn down your job offer later on.

I tend to question more conservatively and mark the answers as I did with the telephone interview - out of five. Questions like these could include:

1. What makes you uniquely suited to this position?
2. Describe a time you went above and beyond.
3. How did you organise your work in your last position?
4. Tell me about a time you overcame a difficult work situation.
5. What does success mean to you?

Etc., etc. Your last question should always be, "Do you have any questions for me?" This gives the interviewee a little more time to find out about you and your company. Crucially, it also lets you have some last-minute insight into the applicant. Questions show the candidate is interested in the position, have researched the organisation, and that they're confident and intelligent enough to think of questions of their own. A "no" in this case indicates that the interviewee can't think for themselves or process new information.

Finally, once I've drawn the cream from the face-to-face interviews, I ask all those who would be a good fit to complete the Kolbe personality test.

The Kolbe Personality Test

The Kolbe RightFit assessment is one of the top career tests that measure a candidate on four traits:

1. **Fact Finder.** This area focuses on acquiring information, then being able to explain, simplify and strategize it.
2. **Follow Thru.** Here, the candidate concentrates on organising, adapting and systemising data.
3. **Quick Start.** This part of the test assesses the candidate's ability to get the job done, particularly measuring their creativity, diversity of thought and ability to cope with sudden change.
4. **Implementer**. On the more visible spectrum, this test measures how a candidate handles space and objects.

These four traits are categorised into three indexes: A, B and C. The A index looks at instinctive characteristics and how well a candidate deals with work-related problems, adapts to change and initiates problem-solving behaviours.

Kolbe Index B highlights a candidate's natural interests and expectations. If you compare A and B together, you can see any problems that may arise when putting an applicant in a particular position.

Lastly, Index C identifies the energy and challenges necessary for effective performance of the job. The candidate whose Index A answers most closely relate to their Index C responses is the right person for the role.

The test is 36 questions and is taken online. Each item is four possible answers, and the candidate needs to rate them 1-4 (1 being "most likely", 4 being "least likely"). Here are a couple of sample questions:

- If I were told to hurry finishing a project, I would
    1. Hurry to finish it
    2. Take my time to get it right
    3. Discuss the rush
    4. Enlist a co-worker to help

- If I were trying to solve a problem, I would depend on my
    1. Experiments
    2. Ability to organise
    3. Skills
    4. Research

Before you administer the Kolbe test, it's vital you know precisely what you're looking for in the role. Obviously, everyone would like someone who's very highly organised, who follows all the rules and still manages to be creative. But, at risk of finding nobody suitable due to over-the-top expectations, just clarify with yourself what values you may rate more than others in one particular job.

For a PPC Manager, for example, theoretically, there are a number of Kolbe scores are possible. However, the traits you need to measure are those that would make a person suitable to be a key player in your firm. Here are a few key skills essential to fulfilling the role:

- Proactivity
- Self-analytical
- Excellent Communication
- Composure
- Willing to take on a variety of challenges
- High levels of organisation
- Desire to learn
- Experts in their field
- Willing to make decisions based on their instincts
- Always one step ahead

You can definitely use a Kolbe test to uncover and explore these traits within your interviewees.

The Kolbe test costs $50, which is much less than the $30,000+ for employing the wrong person and having them leave after a year. You can also customise the test depending on the number of candidates and managers involved in the hiring process.

For a Kolbe test to use on your next set of candidates, please visit this website here:

https://secure.kolbe.com/k2/show_takeIndex/indexType_A.

So, once the test tasks, phone interview, direct interview and Kolbe test are all done, you need to sit down and make a decision. Hopefully, administering the Kolbe test as the finishing touch will have made one candidate stand out beyond the rest. If worse comes to the worst, you can post a second job specification online and start again. Though frustrating and costly, it's better to take your time hiring, be fast to sack a bad fit, and find someone you're completely happy with. You want the very best people for your organisation, so take the time to review and improve your hiring process. It's worth it!

Chapter 4

Building Facebook Campaigns for Great Quality Leads

The Facebook Algorithm

So, way back in Chapter 1, I talked about the miracle of Facebook advertising. On 6th November 2007, Mark Zuckerberg stood in front of a New York audience and introduced Facebook Ads: a system for businesses to connect with users and target advertisements to the exact audiences they want.

At the time, the system was revolutionary. Within a year, 100,000 new Facebook pages launched, covering the world's largest brands, local businesses, organisations and music groups. Users were able to become a "Fan" of that business, "Like" their page, and post comments on the company's "Wall". Any action on behalf of the user would show up in their newsfeed, inviting further comments, pictures or Likes for the company from their friends.

The ad system also served Social Ads that would combine an action from a Facebook friend - like a restaurant review, or a photo of a product - with an advertiser's message. Naturally, the idea behind this was to encourage the user's peers to make a similar purchase or use the company's service. Lots of landmark brands jumped onto this bandwagon, including Blockbuster, Coca-Cola, Microsoft and Sony.

Since 2007, Facebook Advertising has gone through an incredible amount of change. Thanks to feedback from businesses and users alike, constant updates, and its fair share of controversy, the system has transformed from an immature and complicated process to one that operates using Artificial Intelligence, requiring barely any technical knowledge.

It used to be that I would have to sit down with my ad, then trawl through Facebook to find the best gender, the best age and what appeals to a distinct group of people and why. So, for example, when I worked for a car finance company, I would spend hours trying to find prospects interested in family cars, luxury cars, cars better suited to the country, and so on. I'd then have to scale the ad to a particular location or experiment with what time of day netted the biggest audience.

All of that took quite a lot of skill as an agency. It was time-consuming and challenging work, which is why most local businesses (and even some larger companies) tried to outsource these kinds of tasks. It was a brand new, alien experience and many thought it would be best to leave it to the experts.

But, as I mentioned in Chapter 1, the introduction and popularisation of AI in 2014 meant Facebook could remove the responsibilities of researching target markets, insertion orders, budgets and analytical tracking from their business users, and utilise intelligent tools to do it all automatically.

Still, it's not just a case of *upload and go*. Facebook's algorithms require a certain level of knowledge, and new updates mean you'll have to keep on your toes if you want your advertisements to work. Organic marketing has taken a big hit, with Facebook altering its algorithm to reduce the number of spammy posts and blogs that appear in users' feeds. In April 2018, organic reach was at an all-time low, with an average engagement rate of less than 1%.

But there's no need to panic. As with the GDPR changes, Facebook's new algorithm encourages businesses to work smarter, not harder. In reality, all you need to do is make some changes to your content strategy to guarantee the results you need.

Let's go back to the beginning.

What is the Facebook Algorithm?

To put it simply, the Facebook algorithm is a set of calculations that decides what content you see on your newsfeed. At the beginning of Facebook history, newsfeeds tended to be chronological, meaning you'd see an update seconds after it happened. Today, Facebook scans which adverts, articles, statuses and videos are most likely to appeal to you and elicit a response. That's why you'll rarely see a status from the friend you never talk to, or see the same post from another, better, friend three days later. It's like a colleague who repeats a joke after the first attempt didn't get a laugh.

Until early this year, feeds were filled with everything from respectable *Guardian* articles to blog posts from your favourite musician. Then, particularly during the 2016 United States presidential election, the creation and coverage of "fake news" reached its peak. Famed for outlandish headlines and irresistibly clickable stories, fake news fooled millions with outrageous claims and made-up facts. Facebook became a hotbed of false and misleading information, leading to numerous complaints.

As Facebook became more associated with promoting false news stories, certain groups used the platform to push their own agendas. In 2016, the Russian government funded a wave of Facebook political advertisements that targeted American voters. Using Facebook profile information, Russia targeted anything from racial unrest to gun rights to nationalist sentiment to try and sway the upcoming US election. Referred to as the "Russian Ad Scandal", Facebook's reputation took quite a hammering.

In January 2018, Facebook took some huge steps to ensure fake news was wiped from the platform. Mark Zuckerberg announced that the algorithm would, from then on, prioritize "meaningful interactions" from friends and family over content from brands. This meant that a lot of businesses and publishers saw their content get less coverage, as Facebook preferred to serve native posts from users. A loss of coverage meant less traffic which, in turn, meant fewer leads.

After the changes, Matt Navarra, a Social and Digital Media Consultant and self-professed "Facebook geek", released a webinar explaining the new Facebook algorithm and how it works. Here's the information he shared with us.

Facebook's algorithm is separated into four basic components.

- Inventory (content available)
- Signals (considerations about content)
- Predictions (considerations about the person)
- Overall score

These four factors all work together to give users a better overall Facebook experience. Breaking these down, we have:

1. **Inventory.** Self-explanatory. Facebook refers to all available content for a user's feed. This includes posts from friends and family, groups you've joined and pages you like.

2. **Signals.** Facebook now uses signals to select what it thinks the user would most like to read or watch. Some specific signals affecting Facebook rankings include:

   - Comments and likes on a user's status or photo
   - Engagement with publisher content shared by friends
   - Shares on Messenger
   - Replies to comments on a video
   - What time it was posted
   - Content type
   - Average time spent on content
   - How informative the post is
   - Completeness of profile

3. **Predictions.** Facebook uses your profile information and previous behaviour to decide what to show you. They automatically work out how likely you are to engage or interact with content. If the algorithm thinks the user won't like it, they won't bother showing it on the feed.

4. **Score.** Once Facebook has made these decisions, they'll give the content in question a "score". If it's deemed "highly relevant", that will boost the score and the article, ad or video will appear on the person's feed. Obviously, content has a different score for individual users.

Now we've separated and discussed the components of the algorithm, I'm hoping you'll start to see what I mean by working smarter, not harder.

How Does the Algorithm Affect PPC?

Facebook absolutely **can't afford to lose its advertisers.** Mobile advertising accounts for more than 90% of Facebook's revenue growth and drives 88% of the platform's total profit. However cautious and cynical you feel about Facebook advertising, I guarantee that Facebook is prepared to turn cartwheels to keep everyone happy.

The new "meaningful interactions" rule hasn't stopped Facebook from acquiring a tonne of personal data on each and every one of its users. You can still use demographic and personal attributes to target an audience, as well as use Facebook's archive of a person's Likes, shares, posts and uploads.

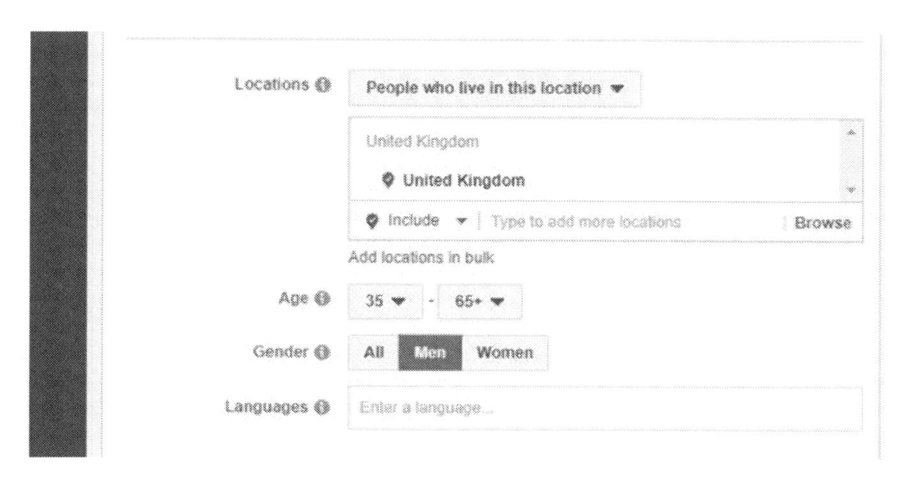

Though this is an example at its most basic, altogether this information can build a solid customer profile. Once you've got some good ads ready to go live, you can layer up your targets to make an audience as niche and specific as you could ever want.

And, once you've found an audience that converts into great-quality leads, you can clone them. This feature is called "lookalike audiences". Facebook will look at the audience you've already got, then target new people who are similar - judging by their Likes, shares, etc. - and likely to be interested in your service or product.

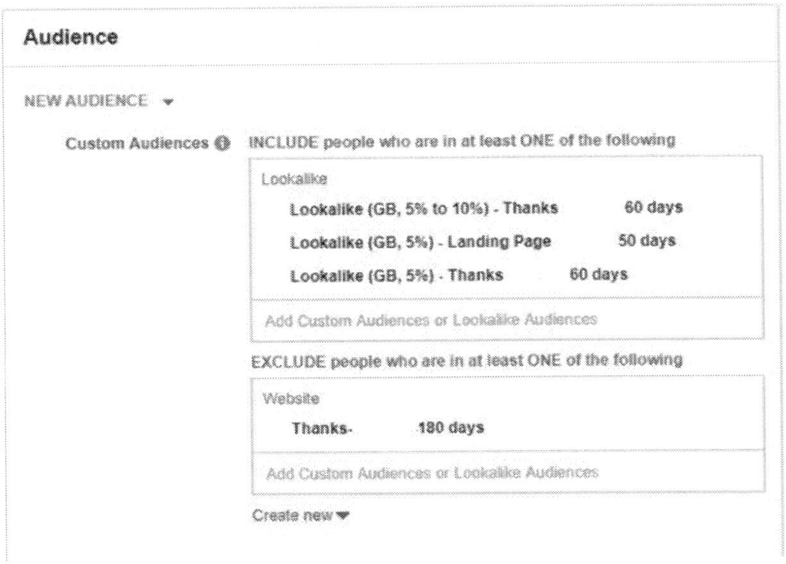

Audience

NEW AUDIENCE

Custom Audiences INCLUDE people who are in at least ONE of the following

Lookalike

Lookalike (GB, 5% to 10%) - Thanks 60 days

Lookalike (GB, 5%) - Landing Page 50 days

Lookalike (GB, 5%) - Thanks 60 days

Add Custom Audiences or Lookalike Audiences

EXCLUDE people who are in at least ONE of the following

Website

Thanks- 180 days

Add Custom Audiences or Lookalike Audiences

Create new

The secret to a successful campaign then is, as I've said before, **knowing your audience and producing great content.**

"Paying to play" guarantees Facebook will show your advertisements, as long as you've scaled them successfully to the right kind of audience. However, the amount of times your ad is shown, or how much money goes on a particular ad, depends entirely on how good your content is and how much your audience is willing to interact with it.

To help you sort which ads are doing better than others, Facebook introduced a Relevance Score metric in February 2015. Equivalent to Google AdWords' Quality Score, the metric measures the ad's effectiveness, how often they should deliver your ad, and the overall cost you pay for the campaign.

The social media platform then uses feedback from ad viewers to determine a score from 1 - 10. 10 is "highly relevant" and the best possible score you can get.

The Facebook Ad Relevance Score

Again, this is self-explanatory.

When scoring your ad, Facebook will take into account both positive and negative feedback. It continues to score your ad on a continual basis, so don't get disheartened too soon. Facebook gives you the score after 500 impressions, but another 200-500 may see your ad climb up the relevance ladder.

Negative feedback could mean a user hiding, ignoring or reporting your ad. Recently, Facebook has also been making use of its "reaction" buttons to determine the quality of content. While hovering can improve an advert's Relevance Score (as it takes a few more precious seconds to "heart" something than it does to like it!), ads that see a spike of angry or annoyed faces may see their Relevance Score consequently dip.

Positive feedback means measuring comments, Likes, positive reactions and shares. Facebook particularly likes it if a user responds with a gif or a video. If your Relevance Score is above 5, Facebook will reward you with a discount for each click. This means more visibility for less cost, and less cost means a higher ROI.

Likewise, while you don't want to judge the Relevance of your ad too soon, you'll also want to keep an eye on it while the going's still good. The score can fluctuate daily, and this is Facebook's way of keeping users' feeds current. If your ad has a Relevance of 8 or 9 one day, then a score of 4 or 5 a week later, it may be time to consider freshening things up.

How To Improve Your Facebook Relevance Score

I keep saying it, but, once again, it's down to knowing your audience and making great ads.

Facebook has so much to offer that people find themselves scrolling blindly through their feed, looking for something that really grabs their attention. For a typical image and text ad, you have about 3 seconds to make an impression. That means picking an image that'll immediately grab your audience, an irresistible headline, and a short subtitle or summary that *always promises more.*

If you've done a good enough job at audience creation, the copy will entice the user into clicking the ad, going through the funnel, and eventually becoming a lead.

It's that simple.

Another way to increase your score is to really **whittle down your audience.** This may sound like you're deliberately sabotaging your own success rate, but think about it.

If you target very specifically, Facebook will ensure that only interested parties will see your offer. Your ad won't reach 1 billion people, but it may result in 200 or 300 conversions. The cost per lead will plummet, leaving you with a very tidy profit.

Then, once your pixel has been "seasoned" with enough conversions from highly-targeted parties, you can start widening your audience again. Because the algorithm now knows exactly what you're looking for, it will automatically target those who may also be interested in your product and/or service from a much wider pool. If you have a highly sought after and nationally appealing offer, this way of targeting can be very effective indeed.

The Facebook Pixel

Okay, so now we're onto the important stuff. If you're going to use Facebook ads, the Facebook pixel is a vital tool you should start using right away to get the most out of your budget. Without the Facebook pixel, you're limiting your target options, can't track conversions accurately and won't be able to optimise for conversions either.

What is a Facebook Pixel?

A Facebook Pixel is a snippet of code you place on your website. It helps you to track conversions from your Facebook ads, optimise ads depending on collected data, build targeted audiences, and remarket to qualified leads - anyone who has taken action on your website.

The pixel works by triggering cookies to track users as they interact with your Facebook ads, funnels and website.

A cookie is a simple text file, typically containing two pieces of information: a site name and a unique user ID. When you visit a site for the first time, a cookie is downloaded onto your PC. When you revisit the site, a cookie "knows" you've been there before and, in some cases, will tailor what you see for a more varied customer experience.

What is a Facebook Pixel for?

1. **Conversion tracking.** The Facebook pixel lets you monitor how people interact with your website after viewing your Facebook ad. You can even track the kind of device customers use, helping you to refine your ad strategy and calculate your ROI.

2. **Remarketing.** The pixel tracking data lets you show targeted ads to users who've already visited your site. Remarketing is the perfect way to really hone your targeting - you can show these people an advertisement for the product they abandoned in their shopping cart or added to a wishlist on your website. Never underestimate the power of remarketing. It's one of the most critical elements of Facebook advertising, and the wealth of opportunities it opens should be used from the outset.

3. **Creating lookalike audiences.** I mentioned lookalike audiences briefly when explaining the Facebook algorithm. With a pixel to track who's visited your site, Facebook can use its targeting data to *automatically* build another audience of users who have similar interests, likes and demographics to those who are currently interacting with your website. This is a very, very useful tool for expanding your potential customer base.

4. **Running effective ads.** The pixel's data will show you who viewed your website and which pages they've clicked as a direct result of your Facebook ad. This is particularly helpful when it comes to **split testing** a set of ads, as you'll be able to see which adverts appeal most to your target audience. You can also use the Facebook pixel to ensure your adverts are seen by the people most likely to take action and buy your product/service.

How To Use a Facebook Pixel

You can use a Facebook pixel to collect data on two different kinds of events: a standard event (defined into 9 separate categories) or a custom conversion event that you've established yourself. An "event" is a specified action that a visitor takes on your website.

For our Facebook campaigns, we tend to use a custom conversion event to ensure Facebook tracks when a user has clicked on the ad, gone through the funnel, and come through to our Thank You page. This way, we know for definite whether we have A) a solid lead and B) how many people failed to convert after clicking onto the funnel.

To use Facebook custom conversions, you'll need to tell Facebook the details of the conversion you want to track. You can do this by **clicking on Facebook Ads Manager**, going to **Custom Conversions** and then clicking on **Create Custom Conversions**.

If you'd rather use one of the nine standard Facebook pixel events, here they are:

- **View content:** This measures the people who land on a page on your website.
- **Search:** A user uses the search function to look for something on your site.
- **Add to cart**
- **Add to wishlist**
- **Initiate checkout:** Someone *starts* to buy, but doesn't complete the purchase
- **Add payment info:** A user enters their payment information in the purchase process on your website

- **Make a purchase**
- **Lead:** Someone signs up for a trial or establishes themselves as a lead on your site
- **Complete registration:** A user fills in a registration form on your website, e.g. for a subscription or repeated service.

As you're looking to generate leads, the final two "events" are probably the most useful for your campaign.

How To Create a Facebook Pixel

- Go on to your Facebook Ads Manager and click the (≡) icon. Select **Pixels.**
- Then click **Create a Pixel.**
- Give your pixel a name and click **Next.** You only get **one pixel** for each ad account, so name the pixel after your business rather than a specific campaign.
- Once you've made your pixel, it'll generate a code. **Copy and paste the code** into the header code of your website - **after the <head> tag but before the </head> tag.** You need to do this on every single page and template.
- Click **Next.**
- **Copy your chosen event code** based on the actions you want to track on your website. For a custom code, click **Custom Event.**
- **Paste the event code in the appropriate location on your webpage** based on the action you've chosen to track. It should go **below the </head> tag** for a new page that opens in response to a tracked action (like a thank you page). Then, click **Next.**

- Then, **download the Facebook Pixel Helper extension for Google Chrome**. This will help you see if your Facebook Pixel is working correctly. You'll be able to see the FPH's icon in the top, right-hand corner of your screen. A number will appear to indicate the number of pixel events. When you click on the icon, you'll be able to see a detailed overview of the page's pixels, including warnings, errors and successes. It's a handy tool!
- If there's an error with your pixel, the Facebook Pixel Helper troubleshooting tool will provide information to help you make corrections.

It's the Facebook pixel that brought an end to difficult, complex advertising campaigns. Once the pixel has collected enough data (e.g. 50+ conversions), you can use the information to manipulate Facebook's algorithm into targeting a wider audience. Say, for instance, your potential audience is 20 million people. With the help of a pixel, Facebook is smart enough to show ads to the tiny segment of that 20 million likely to turn into a lead.

Sounds magical, doesn't it?

How To Create Intrigue Rather Than Sell Your Service

Let's start with a bit of logic.

According to the Oxford English Dictionary, an advertisement is "a notice or announcement in a public medium promoting a product, service or event."

So, going by this dictionary definition, you should be using your Facebook advertisements to promote your products as often as you can, right?

Wrong.

Facebook doesn't follow this kind of logic. Primarily a platform for connecting with family and friends, bragging about how great your life is, and stalking ex-partners, nobody *initially* goes on Facebook to buy anything.

Successful advertising on Facebook isn't so much *upping* your game as changing the game entirely. You're in direct competition with heartfelt statuses, funny posts, holiday snaps and ultrasounds. In theory, people go on Facebook to *learn.* To learn about other people's lives, or to find out about the hot new social trends.

This means your ad, the one that says "BUY THESE SHOES, 50% OFF", is nothing more than an interruptive annoyance. People know when they're being sold something, as it happens to them hundreds of times a day. As a result, they develop something I call "ad blindness" - an intrinsic recognition of all forms of advertising on a subconscious level, allowing them to skip or scroll past without registering the product or service.

Facebook advertising requires a little more stealth. It's like you're tricking a user into reading your advertisement while, simultaneously, being completely open about what you're trying to do.

For example, you may see an article reviewing a new car model. The article will talk about the speed, the engine, the emissions, the upholstery, what it's like to drive etc., etc. All these nuggets of information will layer upon one another until the reader has a sound idea of what the car is like.

Without a call-to-action at the bottom of the page, the reader has just read a really informative article about a particular type of car. And, if that lies in their interest, they may remember that article next time they want to invest in a new set of wheels.

Chances are, you've read this type of article without realising you're looking at an ad.

Let's take another example.

Way back in the 1950s, David Ogilvy, the "Father of Advertising", released an article that took the advertising world by storm: *The Guinness Guide to Oysters.*

Separated into 12 individual "boxes" by a printed grid of knotted rope, each section of the ad contained a picture of a half-shelled oyster. Underneath each oyster was the name of its type in bold, and a short description of its taste and history:

"CAPE CODS: *An oyster of superb flavour. Its chief enemy is the star-fish, which wraps its arms about the oyster and forces the valves open with its feet."*

In the penultimate box was the call-to-action, but a suggestive, rather than a demanding one:

"All oysters taste their best when washed down with drafts of Guinness..."

Then, in the last box of the grid, was a picture of the product: a bottle of Guinness.

While this one was *definitely* an ad, it was so surprising and informative, no one really minded. In fact, it made its readers want to pair oysters with Guinness and see what the combo tasted like.

This is the kind of intrigue you want to create when building your Facebook ads.

On Facebook, you've got a lot less time to hook your prospect. Most of the advert will be dominated by an image, so choose your graphics carefully. Then you've got room for a 4-13 word headline, and 18-80 words to convince the user to make the click. You've got to be able to hint at a *lot* while actually saying very little.
So, let's look at the steps for creating a good ad.

1. Understanding your product or service.

It sounds obvious, but you can't even begin to sell your product or service without understanding it from the inside out. Really pull it apart.

You can even do this with the most boring set of goods on the planet. Take a mop, for example. You know what it does and what it's for, and so does your audience. But you need to be searching for more answers than just "it cleans the kitchen floor".

Why *your* particular mop? What makes it special? (And not something like "we only use the finest fibres". Your audience won't care.) What is it about this mop that subverts the usual expectations of a cleaning appliance?

It's only when you really understand your product you can hope to come up with a good hook. Ask yourself every "stupid" question in the book. If the problem occurs to you, it will occur to your readers/viewers too.

2. Hook with your headline

You've got about three seconds and 18-80 words to make the user click your ad. How do you want to draw people to you? You have several options available:

- **Start with a question.** Is there a "surprise" element to your product or service? Or perhaps something immediately beneficial? You could phrase your headline as an open-ended question to spark your audience's curiosity. In February 2018, DashThis, an agency reporting software company, asked Facebook, *"What's the difference between DashThis and a regular old spreadsheet?"*

- Although DashThis' service isn't one anybody would call "terrifically exciting", they managed to take something very dull (a spreadsheet) and, in turn, suggested their product (also a bit boring) is more exciting than the original object. In the space of a question, DashThis tapped into three selling points:

  - ➔ **Inevitability:** Spreadsheets are just a part of life
  - ➔ **Intrigue:** Our automated spreadsheets are somehow different, and you can find out why
  - ➔ **Promise/Solution:** By being different, our product is *better*. This could be the *solution* to your "boring spreadsheet" problem

- **Make a statement that promises more information.** Earlier this year, one of my copywriters, Graham Connolly, wrote an advert for Aunt Meg, our debt advice service especially for mums. His headline was clear and straight to the point: *"How mums are writing up to 75% off their debt."*

Debt has no glitz or glamour, and neither did the hook. He didn't try to fool anyone with clever wordplay or mislead anyone with false statements (he never claimed *all* their debt was written off). Instead, he tapped into the same three selling points:

- ➔ **Inevitability:** People get into debt and have to pay it back
- ➔ **Intrigue:** How did these mums get so much debt written off?
- ➔ **Promise/Solution:** Read the article, find out how, and you can do the same

- **Use a short testimonial.** In March 2018, The Paleo Secret, a dietary website, posted an advert promoting their new 30-day paleolithic diet. The headline read: *"***** 'The 30 Day Challenge is AMAZING.'"*

  Amazing is an evocative word, and the fact it appears in a (very short and to the point) testimonial inspires faith in the service. Again, there's no trickery or wordplay, it just dives straight into the heart of the matter:

  - ➔ **Inevitability:** People need to diet if they want to feel good
  - ➔ **Intrigue:** Diets are usually horrible. Why is this one "amazing"?
  - ➔ **Promise/Solution:** 30 days isn't very long. It's a manageable solution for a healthy lifestyle.

- **Be negative.** Yes, really! If all else fails, take your ad and give it a cynical spin. According to a study on Outbrain.com, negative headlines perform 30% better than positive ones, and receive a 69% higher click-through rate!

Though this may sound surprising, the psychology behind it is quite simple. Think of a newspaper. Would you rather read an article headlined *"Children Have Summer Fun in the Park"*, or *"Murderous Ex-Girlfriend's Cannibalistic Revenge"*?

Humans prefer to read something that taps into the fours S's:
Shock
Shame
Surprise
Strong emotional response (empathy, anger, fear, etc.)

The ad world is also glutted with superlatives, making sales-pitches sound disingenuous. Everything's sold as "astonishing" or "fabulous" or "groundbreaking" and, most of the time, the products turn out to be OK at best.

Here are some examples of good "negative" headlines:

- ➔ 7 Reasons Your Marketing Agency is Destined To Fail (confrontational)
- ➔ One Small Mistake Means This Mum is $200,000 in Debt (scare tactics)
- ➔ How Lindsay Lohan Destroyed Her Looks (taps into insecurity, newsworthy)

You'll also notice that these negative headlines all deliver on the Inevitability/Intrigue/ Promise fronts. Overall, the message is: learn about these people, don't do what they do, and you'll be fine.

3. Remember EVERY word counts

For your Facebook advert, you'll need to write some compelling copy directly underneath the headline and in the summary box above. Facebook recommends that the text doesn't go beyond 125 characters.

This is a guideline, not a rule, though brevity works best when hooking your audience.

The main thing is to keep it to the point. This is your chance to pull in customers after they've digested the headline - the little extra push they need to click on the ad. Stay away from clever wordplay or wandering from the subject.

Refine everything as much as possible. Take out any unnecessary adjectives, and replace longer words with shorter ones. **And make sure the words make sense!**

In February this year, Prevention Magazine released a Facebook ad for Palmer's, a popular beauty brand that specialises in cocoa butter infused products. The headline stated, *"5 Tips To Say Good-bye To Winter Skin"*, with the copy reading: *"So long, winter beauty blahs! #ad"*.

This was a confusing and disappointing ad for such a big company. Because the creative was focused on the *wordplay,* (aka the alliteration of "beauty" and "blahs") they failed to engage with the brand or resonate with an audience. The headline was OK, feeding into the idea of a listicle, but it was badly worded and made little sense on a second reading. The unnecessary "#ad" was the final nail in the coffin.

In contrast, a PPI advert written by my PPC Manager, Gavin Miles, has performed very successfully on Facebook.

The headline is straight to the point, promising to solve a problem known by many - the uncomfortable wait on the telephone, the hold music, the stilted conversation.

The copy is straightforward and speaks directly to its audience. There's no "hard sell" - it's a statement worded carefully to spark curiosity. The emojis are a smart choice; they help to "humanise" a financial service, with Facebook reporting that emoji use can increase Likes, comments and shares by up to 57%.

4. Always test your ads

No ad is perfect, and ones you think will do brilliantly can disappoint you when they're up online. Always be prepared to analyse what works well and why.

We use split-testing as a way to try out different approaches with the ads. It's a great way to study the effects of copy variation and which style resonates most with your target audience. A split-test also has the advantage of producing data within a few hours, letting you fail fast and fix the problem even faster.

When you write your next piece of ad copy, keep these tips in mind. They will help you refine your social media advertisements and produce better results. They'll also help you with the next stage of your funnel: The Advertorial.

How Advertorials Work

In the previous section, I wrote about creating ads that entertain and build intrigue. The next part of the process is what we call a funnel. A funnel primes the prospect after they've made the initial click on an ad. It gently encourages them to learn more about the product or service, gain confidence in it, and make a step towards a purchase.

I'll give you an example. Let's look at the PPI advertisement I used before.

Imagine if you clicked on that ad, and it took you straight to a landing page, asking for your name, telephone number and email address. Something would seem off, right? Even the promise of a free consultation seems suspect if you know nothing about the company, its services, or the solutions it offers.

Hell hath no fury like a reader scorned. If a user feels like they've been misled, or the advert doesn't provide the information it promises, they'll flag your work as spam.

A reader will always want to know more about the product or service and, from that, they'll judge whether your company is legitimate. The best way to do this, I've found, is through an advertorial or pre-sales page.

I spoke briefly about advertorials in Chapter 1. Once your audience has clicked on the ad out of curiosity, they've now moved onto to the second phase of purchasing: consideration.

Much like your Facebook ad, the object of this exercise *isn't* to start walloping your prospects with a hardcore sales pitch. Think of an advertorial like a slow seduction. You'd take them out, talk to them, make them laugh and show off your numerous charms. You definitely wouldn't propose, sweating and fumbling, on the first date.

This slow seduction usually takes the form of about 500 to 1000 words. Any longer and you'll risk the reader getting bored. With so few words, you'll need to craft an advertorial with the same care as you would a short story.

Advertisers are becoming increasingly aware of the impact of a well-crafted advertorial, with sponsored posts expected to generate $21 billion in revenue this year - a huge leap in comparison to the $4.7 billion earned in 2013.

But what makes a good advertorial and how can you use it to convert more customers?

1. **Create high-quality content that's relevant to your product/service.** I've mentioned this point a lot, and it's always the key to a successful advertorial. Don't let your work become sloppy just because you're using an extended format! Every word counts.

2. **Let the headlines do the hard work.** Just as you did with the Facebook ad, you'll need to sit down and think hard about your headline. Your goal is to make the advertorial look like an article or feature, so leave any elaborate wordplay out of the mix.
   That's not to say the headline shouldn't be clever. It needs to be interesting, compelling and unexpected. In November 2013, The Tulsa World, a newspaper distributed in Oklahoma, released an article with the following headline and subheading:

   Headline: *Public lines up for new low-cost appliance that slashes heat bills*

   Subheading: *Amish craftsmen vow to keep up with rush for brand new Hybrid-Thermic 'Miracle Heater' that uses about the same energy as a coffee-maker per hour, so just plug it in and never be cold again.*

   Ouch. This advertorial had gone to great lengths to look like a genuine news article, with a large photograph of people queuing outside Sears, an American department store. However, a headline that proclaims "slashes heat bills" may as well have #UlteriorMotive written next to it. "So plug it in and never be cold again" has been lazily crowbarred into the subheading, essentially giving away the entire point of the article before the prospect has had a chance to read it. That's 500 wasted, ineffective words.

Like any good sales strategy, your headline needs to generate a thirst to find out more and keep the prospect reading.

One advertorial that still excites marketers is John Caple's US School of Music advertisement, written in 1926. Developed during Caple's first year at Ruthrauff & Ryan, the headline reads:

"They Laughed When I Sat Down At the Piano... But When I Started to Play!~"

As a headline, it worked brilliantly. There's no hard-sell or overload of information. Instead, the success lies in the emotion it stirs up within the reader. From a few words, we can tell this is a classic "underdog reaches the spotlight" story, and we want to know how and why it happened. The body of the copy is written like short fiction, from "Jack's" point of view. He explains how he sat down at the piano at a party, only to be mocked by his friends and acquaintances, who knew he'd never played the piano in his life. After a flawless rendition of the *Moonlight Sonata,* however, the other guests burst into "a sudden roar of applause". The story then filters down to its call-to-action, promising the US School of Music's ability to teach anyone how to play any instrument in only a few months.

3. **Relate your message to real life.** Another reason Caple's advertorial did so well is that he bought a relatable character to the page: Jack. In only a few hundred words, Jack's entire personality was brought forward to an audience of thousands. He's a charming, easy-going "everyman"; a bit

of a clown, the guy everyone underestimates... until he reveals his hidden talents. Everybody sees themselves in Jack, and will be keen to emulate his success.

It all comes down to the difference between pointing out a feature and a benefit.

A feature is what your product or service does. Taking a real example from my own ad campaigns in FlexxDigital, let's look at the debt advice service, Aunt Meg.

Aunt Meg's features are that the service will offer you a government-approved way of getting out of debt without declaring bankruptcy. This is usually via an Individual Voluntary Arrangement (IVA) which lets you pay off your debt in instalments. If the debt isn't paid off by the time the IVA ends (typically after 60 months), you could end up writing off a portion of your debt.

Though this explanation is A) factually correct and B) what the customer is ultimately looking for, there are hundreds of services that provide exactly the same features. What we need to do, then, is to relate our message to real life and point out all the benefits. This will put us ahead of other debt advice companies, as we'll be humanising the service and speaking directly to the customer.

A benefit is something of value and usefulness. It takes the feature and explains why it'll be useful for you, as a human being. By describing the benefits, you're offering a solution to a customer's needs, wants, and fears.

Going back to Aunt Meg, it's pretty easy to see what the benefits are from looking at the website, auntmeg.com. Aunt Meg is a character branded as "your financial fairy godmother with attitude", meaning she'll offer the customer "no-nonsense" advice and a solution to a life imprisoned by debt.

Aimed primarily at mothers, the first paragraph on the landing page reads: "Aunt Meg helps mums sort out their debts. Leaving time for you to relish in the important stuff - your kids." Instead of going for an IVA hard-sell, Aunt Meg takes a very human situation and tackles the emotions borne from it. Being in debt can be stressful and time-consuming. You may be so worried about paying bills and keeping the bailiffs from your door, you don't have the energy or emotional capacity to focus on your children. Aunt Meg can help with that and give you back the life you deserve.

For a successful advertorial, you need to talk about why the benefits of a product or service are significant, what they can do to help, and how they will change the customer's life for the better.

If you're having trouble thinking of the benefits of your product/service, here's a tip I learned from Dave Dee, a key figure in sales training. List a feature, followed by the clause *"which is useful because"*, then add the benefit. For example:

This book contains instructions on how to write an advertorial *which is useful because* you'll be able to build a high-converting funnel, ensuring great quality leads and a better ROI.

4. **Use images, photos and quotes.** Even if your advertorial is beautifully written, there's nothing more boring than a huge block of text. Use pictures to break up the wall of

writing, and make sure they're relevant to your service or product. Remember, an image can set the tone as much as writing style - so don't use a meme if your content is written like a newspaper article.

Quotes are also a great way to grab a reader's attention. You can use testimonials, opinions, or facts. Quotes will lend your product or service a sense of authenticity, which could be the difference between your customer choosing to buy or looking elsewhere.

5. **Use a subtle call-to-action.** If the main body of the copy is like a slow seduction, then the last paragraph or so should suggest a second date. Be careful not to switch from an editorial style into hard-hitting business speak. This will disconcert the reader and may cause them to drop out. Subtly weave in the name of your product or service throughout the article and plant the seed that will result in a sale. At the very end, tell your readers what to do and where they need to go. This will increase the chance of converting a prospect into a lead by 70%.

6. **Always split-test your advertorials.** There's no knowing what will appeal to your audience until you split-test a variety of options. A beautifully written newspaper-style article may capture a different type of audience to a listicle, and you should take the opportunity to experiment with various styles, images and formats. You never know - you may be onto a winner and just need to change a word or two in the headline. There's a way to easily split-test in Unbounce, managed by duplicating your existing page and making changes to your copy. From here, you'll be able to assign traffic to the variant by clicking the weight percentage and adjusting it how you'd like. You'll only have one URL for the two or more pages - Unbounce will

randomly select which page a visitor sees by your traffic weighting. If your variant is outperforming your current "champion" page, you'll be able to promote the variant to become the new champion! For more information, visit Unbounce's documentation pages, specifying "How to Run an AB Test".

7. **Make sure you have a retargeting code placed on all your pages throughout the funnel.** This is so you can automatically run retargeting ad campaigns throughout Facebook and the rest of the web to bring visitors (who may be more receptive now they've seen another ad) back into your sales funnel process.

Once you've got the art of the advertorial down, you're almost ready to start running successful Facebook campaigns of your very own. But before you leap towards your computer, keep in mind there's more than one way to skin a cat. I wouldn't be able to finish this Facebook chapter without mentioning video as a crucial marketing tool, so turn the page and see the massive selling benefits it can offer.

For an example of one of our successful advertorials (and a landing page!), type the following links into Google:

https://bit.ly/2S5cwOZ - advertorial

https://bit.ly/2MXqlA9 - landing page

Feel free to use these pages as inspiration for your own! We'll show you how to create beautiful looking pages like these in Chapter 5.

The Magic of Facebook Video

While the art of writing a good advertisement isn't one that should be lost to the ages, video is a real stride towards marketing modernity.

Facebook is having something of a love affair with video, with users clocking up 32 billion views a day. In fact, native video posts get more reach than any other kind of content on the social media platform. Facebook has set its algorithm to prioritise video posts, so adverts using this kind of strategy are likely to get greater visibility.

87% of online marketers use video content. If your business is part of the 13% who don't, you run a real risk of being left behind.

People want visuals, audio clips and colours that can capture their imagination. With Facebook's ingenious autoplay feature, the animated screen is more eye-catching than the usual text post. Most users stop and watch an autoplay video for 4-10 seconds as they scroll down their feed.

So, as a business looking to reach a whole new audience and take advantage of Facebook's best marketing tool, how do you craft the perfect video?

How To Capture Your Audience Using Facebook Video

1. **Keep it short.** With so many ideas flying around, it's tempting to create the next Tarantino epic. However, if your budget can stretch to *that*, it's best to make a series of shorter videos instead.

   Short, yet emotive, videos keep your marketing content fresh and provide a stream of entertainment for your fans.

It's also the shorter videos that are more likely to go viral. Facebook itself suggests that videos shouldn't be any longer than 2 minutes - just enough time to send the core message of your brand.

2. **Educate your audience.** Your video should work in a similar way to an advertorial. It's not about blowing up the screen with a hardcore sales-pitch, but leading the prospect gently by the hand towards a purchase.

   Invest in the *story.* This doesn't necessarily mean you need to spend weeks storyboarding an idea with a huge budget and a heartwarming message. The story could just be you, facing the camera, and telling the audience about your company. Let the prospect know how your services can benefit them, and what action they'll need to take. Don't be afraid to add emotion or humour; used correctly, this will only help your case.

3. **Grab their attention within 4 seconds.** 65% of people who watch the first 4 seconds of a Facebook video will watch for at least 10 seconds. This means it's critical to maximise the potential of your video. Make sure it shows something interesting in the opening seconds to prevent viewers from scrolling past. Use graphics, share a joke or ask the viewers a direct question.

4. **Be entertaining.** Just because you're trying to deliver a message, it doesn't mean the video has to be boring. A sign of a great marketer is the ability to take something dull and make it appeal to a worldwide audience.

   On the other hand, "entertaining" doesn't always mean "random". If you think a video of a dog riding a bicycle will help your sales, go ahead and make the upload. If you'd rather make your broadcasts a little more on topic, there's a whole host of ways to grab your audience's attention.

i. 'How to' videos demonstrating a task
ii. Behind-the-scenes videos, featuring the "softer side" of your company
iii. Product or service demonstrations
iv. Customer testimonials
v. Short animations

5. **Add captions to your video.** 85% of Facebook videos are watched without sound. Adding captions could do wonders when pulling in an audience.

6. **Don't forget your call-to-action.** You could post the best video in the world, but without a call-to-action, you may as well be talking into empty space. Facebook allows admins to choose from a range of call-to-action buttons, which will appear at the bottom left-hand side of your video advertisement. These are:

i. Book Now
ii. Contact Us
iii. Use App
iv. Play Game
v. Shop Now
vi. Sign Up
vii. Watch Video

All these are pretty self-explanatory, and admins can edit the button to link to another page on or outside of Facebook (preferably to your advertorial or landing page!)

7. **Upload your videos directly to Facebook.** Native Facebook videos have 186% more engagements than videos linked from other hosting platforms (CoSchedule). Uploading your video directly makes it easier for Facebook's algorithm to put it in front of an interested audience.

   However, bear in mind that Facebook videos have a shorter shelf-life. In a packed newsfeed, once the video stops receiving Likes, shares and comments, it'll travel down the algorithm's list of priorities until it disappears into the ether. If you want to ensure your videos have a longer lifespan, it could be worth uploading them to YouTube too.

It's absolutely crucial to include Facebook video in your content marketing plans. It doesn't require a massive budget, and some videos filmed from a smartphone have proved as successful as those done with a professional camera. As of 2019, 80% of all consumer internet traffic will come from videos on social media. With results like these, the desire to get in on the Facebook video act should be a no-brainer.

Building Your Campaigns

Firstly, let me congratulate you for coming this far. I hope you've learned a lot about the art of Facebook mastery and are comfortable moving forward.

We've got to the bit you've all been waiting for: building your very own Facebook campaigns, entirely in-house.

Before you even start posting your campaign on Facebook, you need to ensure the sales funnel is perfect. Check that your advertorial, lander and thank you page are all performing correctly, optimised for mobile viewing and that the footer has the correct information (to see how to do this, proceed to Chapter 5).

When you're happy with that, you can move on and start creating your Facebook campaign.

The 3 Elements of a Facebook Campaign

Facebook's campaign structure contains three levels:

1. **A Facebook campaign.** Your campaign is essentially a container to help you better organise your advertising. It's at the campaign level where you realise your singular objective. So, if you wanted to convert prospects into leads AND increase the amount of your website traffic, you'd have to set up two individual campaigns.

2. **A Facebook Ad Set.** An Ad Set can contain multiple ads, and they are easy to organise via targeting, budget, schedule, bidding and placement. Ad Sets are the best place to use for split-testing your advertisements, so remember to always place all the variations inside your different ad sets.

3. **The Facebook ad.** This is the smallest unit of your campaign. Ads can use different URLs, images and copy.

Facebook Ads Manager

Now Facebook has dispensed with Power Editor, setting up a campaign is much easier with Facebook Ads Manager. With this free tool, you can:

- Set up Facebook ad campaigns
- Create new ad sets and ads

- Manage Facebook ad bids
- Target lots of different audiences
- Optimise your ad campaigns
- Keep track of your campaigns' performance
- Split-test

To access Facebook Ads Manager, you'll need a Facebook Business Manager account. You can set one up by going to business.facebook.com and marrying the account to your personal page. Facebook Business Manager will give you full access to all your ad accounts, the pages you access, and the primary page you choose to advertise through.

To sign up for Business Manager, follow these steps:

1. Go to **business.facebook.com**
2. Click **Create Account**
3. Enter the name of your company, select the primary page, then fill in your name and work email address
4. Enter in the rest of the required fields - Facebook will walk you through this

How To Add an Ad Account

Now you've got Facebook Business Manager, you should have automatic access to Facebook Ads Manager.

All new businesses are able to create one ad account. Once there is active spend on your ad account, you can host a maximum of five accounts. Unfortunately, there's currently no option to request additional accounts.

If you want to manage an ad account, there are three ways to add the ad account to your Business Manager:

1. Open your **Business Settings.** Select which Business Manager you'd like to work on.
2. Go to **Ad Accounts**
3. On the righthand side of the page, click **Add New Ad Accounts**
4. Choose one of the three options: **Add Ad Account, Request Access to an Ad Account** or **Create a New Ad Account**
5. If you choose to request access or add an ad account, enter the ad account ID. You can do that by going into Ads Manager and clicking the Account drop-down menu. You should then see the ID number for your ad account

Note: Deactivating an ad account doesn't delete it from your business. A deactivated ad account still counts towards your ad account limit.

For a little more clarification on the three ways to add an ad account:

1. **Add an Ad Account:** Adding an Ad Account moves it permanently to Business Manager. You must both be the owner and an admin in Business Manager to add the ad account. Please note, once you add an account and it's moved into your Business Manager, this action can't be reversed. All management of your ad account must be completed within your Business Manager profile. You can't add an account that's owned by another Business Manager. If you want to work on an ad account that's held by a different Business Manager, you can request access to it.

2. **Request Access to an Ad Account:** If you request access to an ad account in Business Manager, the admin of that Business Manager can grant you permission to work on it.

3. **Create a New Ad Account:** If you create a new ad account in Business Manager, it'll permanently belong to that particular manager. Once created within Business Manager, it can't be transferred to an individual owner who doesn't own a Business Manager.

And, if you can't add an ad account to a Business Manager, it means:

1. The ad account you're trying to add has already been added by another business. An ad account can only be owned by one Business Manager. Instead, you can request access to the ad account.

2. You have already added a personal account ad to Business Manager. You can only add one account from your personal Facebook page into Business Manager. Instead, you can create a new ad account in Business Manager, or you can request access to another one.

3. You've reached the five ad account limit for adding new ad accounts to your business. There's currently no option to request additional accounts. Your ad account limit increases based on your advertising spend.

Adding a Payment Method to Business Manager

You must be an admin or a Finance Editor to make any changes to payment methods connected to a Business Manager.

You can add a payment method to your Business Manager to manage all of your billing details in one place. Once you add a payment method to Business Manager, you can add it to an ad account you've connected to Business Manager and then use it as the primary payment method for your ads.

To add a payment method to Business Manager, you must:

1. Open Business Settings
2. Click Payments
3. Select Add Payment Method
4. Click Continue, then follow the instructions provided

Your payment method will be saved to your Business Manager.

To connect a payment method from Business Manager to an existing ad account:

1. Go to Business Manager
2. Click Business Manager in the top navigation and hover over All Tools
3. Click Billing
4. If you have multiple ad accounts, choose which ad account you want to work on in the top-left of Ads Manager
5. Click Payment Settings
6. In the Payment Method section, click Add Payment Method
7. Choose the payment method you added in Business Manager and follow the instructions to add your payment method

After you've added your payment method from Business Manager, make sure it's the primary payment method of your ad account to use it to pay for your ads.

Creating a New Google Tag Manager

A new Google Tag Manager is needed for each client to add relevant pixel codes. It acts as a container within which we add our tracking pixels from other software.

- If you already have a Google Tag Manager account, sign in and skip to the next step.
- If you do not already have a Google Tag Manager account, go to www.google.com/analytics/tag-manager/
- Click 'Sign Up for Free'
- Follow the on-screen instructions
- Once you're set up, click Create Account
- Use company name as an account name
- Use web address/company name as container name
- Select Web
- Create and accept terms of service
- Open notepad
- When "Install Google Tag Manager" pops up - copy and paste both codes plus instructions into notepad

You can see more about Facebook Pixels and Unbounce in Chapter 5 of this book.
Now you've got everything just about set up, you can move onto making the campaign properly.

Campaign Creation

Typically, when we start a new campaign on Facebook, we create a new ad account or use an existing one. From here, we create two campaigns: one will go straight to the landing page, and the other will go to an advertorial.

For a campaign going to a landing page, you'll usually get more leads but of lesser quality. An advertorial, on the other hand, generates fewer leads, but they tend to have a far higher contact rate.

Within each campaign, there will be four ad sets, all with different targeting (i.e. age, interests, mobile phone usage, placements on Facebook and Instagram, etc.).

For each ad set, you'll need to decide the following:

1. **The Objective.** At the campaign level, you choose the action you want people to take when they see your ads. Facebook has three objective categories: Awareness, Consideration and Conversion. The one you select depends entirely on your strategy. In this case, you may think we opt for conversion. In actuality, we use Consideration, then click the Lead Generation option. This is so we can measure customers who have landed on the thank you page - meaning that they've become leads.

2. **Building Your Audience.** This second stage moves to the ad set, which specifies how your ad will run. Targeting is an essential element of your ads' success, so it's vital you get it right. On Facebook, you've got three ways to define your audience.

i. **Target Demographics and Interests.** This is the easiest way to target your audience, and is used for people who haven't previously interacted with your business. Here, you can choose demographic constraints, such as location, age, gender and language.

   If you want to get a bit more detailed, move onto the Detailed Targeting section. This will supply a list of thousands of interests, behaviours and demographics.

   You can also opt for a more "layered" approach by using the AND condition. Click Narrow Audience and select from a variety of life events, financial variables and purchase behaviours.

   You can find all your customer's interests by referring to your Customer Avatar (as mentioned in Chapter 1, The Miracle of Facebook Advertising). An avatar will make you think hard about your prospect's hopes, wants and needs, and will make choosing the right demographics much easier.

ii. **Target a Custom Audience.** A custom audience is a group of people who have already had some interaction with your business on Facebook, website, or email marketing. Using a custom audience is an excellent way of gently inviting "warm prospects" back into considering your product or service.

   When you create a custom audience, you can choose from four categories: Customer File, Website Traffic, App Activity and Engagement on Facebook.

With the Customer File option, you need to upload or import a data list. Facebook will then cross-match the people on your list and find them on Facebook. If you have an existing subscriber list, you can specifically target that audience with your Facebook ad campaigns.

The Website Traffic option is also beneficial. For this kind of audience, you use the Facebook Pixel and conversion tracking to track visitors and their actions. You can create different custom audiences depending on the pages people visited, how long they stayed and what steps they took.

We don't use App Activity very often, but it may be relevant to you. This type of audience allows you to target people who've completed a specific action on your app or online game.

The Engagement Custom Audience type includes people who have interacted with your content on Facebook. Inside this audience option, you can choose from four types of engagement: Video, Lead Ad, Canvas and Page. All these are self-explanatory. A Lead Ad audience, for example, will target people who have explicitly interacted with your lead advertisements.

iii. **Target a Lookalike Audience.** These audiences continuously deliver the best results. Facebook takes the data points from a previous audience you've used and finds new, similar people using a set percentage sample of the population in your chosen country. We usually target the top 10% of people who match, with the top 1% being almost equal counterparts. With lookalike audiences, you can also exclude your customs, meaning you won't target people who have already become leads.

To create a conversion lookalike audience, go to the Audiences dashboard in your Facebook Ads Manager. Click Create Audience, then Custom Audience from the drop-down menu. In the pop-up box, click Website Traffic.

From that drop-down menu, select Custom Combination. Then click the URL drop-down menu and select Event.

Choose the event you want to create the audience from (in this case, it'll probably be Lead). You'll see a full list of event actions you're tracking with your Facebook pixel.

In the Last field, enter the time you want for people to stay in your audience. This can be anything from days to months. Then make sure you've selected the Include Past Website Traffic box, give your audience a name, and click Create Audience.

To start building, go over to the Audiences dashboard, click Create Audience, and select Lookalike Audience from the drop-down menu.

In the Create a Lookalike Audience box, choose your named website custom audience from the Source list.

Select your country and choose your audience size. As I said, we prefer anything between 1 - 10%.

Click Create Audience, sit back and wait. Once Facebook has built your lookalike, it'll appear in your Audiences dashboard.

3. **Build and Test Your Ad Creative.** This is the ad level and the last stage of the campaign structure. This is the part your audience will see. Here, you can choose your ad format and creative, including videos, images, news feed text, the display link and the call-to-action button.

   What your Facebook ad looks like depends on your strategy, objective and format. You can choose from five different formats: single video, single image, slideshow, canvas (combining pictures and videos) and carousel (2 or more scrollable images or videos). By creating multiple ads, you can test variations in copy, imagery and overall ad format. This means you can split test and introduce new ads when the relevance score of your current set of ads decreases.

Optimising Your Facebook Ads

You should always have a goal "cost per lead" in mind when starting your campaign and look to optimising your ads as soon as possible.

Always allow time for testing but, after a couple of days, you'll start to get a picture of which ads and ad sets are resonating most with audiences.

If some ads are too expensive to run and are inflating the Cost Per Action (CPA), you should turn them off as soon as you can. You only want the ads with the cheapest CPA turned on during your campaign.

If no ads are performing and reaching your target CPA, even after a variety of split tests, then you'll need to start generating new ads to reach your target.

Both the relevance score AND the Cost Per Click (CPC) are essential when judging your ads' performance. So, if your relevance scores are above 7 and the CPC is below $1, then ads have potential. If they aren't gaining any leads, but these Key Performance Indicators (KPIs) are high, you might want to look at optimising your sales funnel by testing out new landing pages and advertorials.

Chapter 5

Creating a Sales Funnel For High Quality Leads

Why Isn't My Website Converting?

You've written your advertorials.

You've created a winning set of ads.

Your campaign is finally up and running.

There's just one problem. No matter what you do, your website just isn't converting. It's like you're trying to draw water with a sieve.

In this day and age, companies can no longer get away with having a website that acts as an extended business card. Your site needs to be designed and built in a way that captures those leads and optimises the number of people coming into your sales funnel from the website traffic you generate.

The problem is that most businesses owners don't understand traffic and conversion. This means that, when it comes to briefing a website design agency, they're not building the website in a way that generates as many leads as possible. Essentially, it's not a tool that'll last for years - or even months - down the line.

To be fair, it's not only the business owner's fault. They've paid a specialist thousands of dollars, in good faith, to design a good website that'll attract business. Unfortunately, these web designers are not in the game of lead generation, converting visitors, conversion rate optimisation or any of the other things a business owner has been studying for years. A web designer is focused on taking the information they've been given and displaying it in a way they think looks good, so you can't really blame them for bad conversions either.

Instead of playing the "blame game", it's time to start heading towards a solution.

I could say that your best option is to hire another specialist web designer. You *could* spend another $20,000, $30,000 or even up to $50,000 for a site that will take over six months to build and get live.

Doesn't sound that tempting, does it? In reality, most company owners don't have that kind of money just lying around. They certainly don't have the luxury of waiting for six months, unless they're willing to gamble their business won't wither and die before then.

If you're having these problems, you're not alone. I used to find it incredibly overwhelming when we were generating website traffic and pointing it to our clients' websites, simply because we had no control over the process. It was easy to deliver great quality clicks and high-quality traffic to the website, but we weren't able to influence the business owner into making changes quickly. Depending on the size of the company, these changes had to go through the marketing department, then the IT department, and usually an external web designer as well. This could take *weeks.* It just wasn't sustainable.

So, instead of struggling ever forward through mediocrity, we started looking for a real solution. We spent some time researching the market and came across a tool called Unbounce.

Finding this site was like feasting on manna straight from heaven. This tool meant my agency could design beautiful-looking websites and pages, all easily uploadable to our clients' websites via a subdomain. We could finally bypass the chaos with the IT department and the marketing managers and the people with the long trousers that need to sign-off everything.

We can build the landing pages we need to convert the traffic into leads by designing it independently to the website and attaching the page as a subdomain.

The good news, then, is if you have a website you're not happy with at the moment, you can keep it as it is. Sure, you could make a few tweaks to the homepage but, as a whole, you need to start thinking about driving traffic to an internal page.

I'll show you how to make these later on in the chapter.

All this can be done relatively cheaply. Unbounce has a 30-day free trial and starts from as little as $79 per month (if you pay annually). All plans include "Drag and Drop Builder", "Popups and Sticky Bars", "High-Converting Templates" and "Essential Integrations".

It's a handy tool to have because it saves you so much time and money. Once you've got used to the platform, you could have a brand-new website up and running within a few hours. Best of all, anyone with half a brain and a penchant for design can use it.

It is, quite literally, a drag-and-drop website designer, that requires *no* effort, *no* technical skills and *no* coding knowledge.

I'll walk you through it all in the next subchapter: The Power of Unbounce.

The Power of Unbounce

When I first started out in digital marketing and lead generation, I was absolutely terrified of building my own website.

Sound slightly hyperbolic? I wish that were the case. I knew all too well the things that could go horribly wrong.

It was one of the things I put into my "too difficult, don't even try" mental basket after I tried and failed at designing my own WordPress site. My tinkering ended up devaluing my brand. The resulting site looked shoddy, the artwork clashed, and it had nowhere near the amount of professionalism I'd both imagined and required.

The other option for me back then would be to invest a five-figure sum with a local web designer to build my website for me. Unfortunately, as a fledgling business, I didn't have that kind of money.

So, I soon found myself in an awkward situation. Unable to spend any money on creating the site I desperately needed, I was stuck showing the website I designed to my clients. Their reactions said it all.

There I was, trying to prove I was a big player in the lead generation field, selling my services with a website looking like it was built by a sulky teenager in fifteen minutes. Clients who seemed interested would tell me they were looking elsewhere days later, apparently after researching my company.

I needed to find something or someone to help me make that change.

Now, if you happen to take a look at our two websites, www.flexdigital.com (which is our lead generation agency) and www.flexxable.com (our education hub), you will see beautiful and professional-looking pages which have been built on an invaluable platform called Unbounce (www.unbounce.com). This is a drag-and-drop website builder, and I've made substantial use of it for the past three years.

A large part of my websites' success is down to my Graphic and Web Design Manager, Alan Cotter. After choosing to leave his initial career path, he came to me and started an apprenticeship in 2015. With zero coding experience or knowledge, Alan has been designing websites and funnels using Unbounce ever since. Able to assemble a "first draft" for a website or landing page in just a few hours, clients have been unfailingly impressed with his results.

If anyone reading this book is worried about spending a lot of money on a website, I seriously recommend you look at this tool.

Using Unbounce to Create Sales Funnels

When I talk about how FlexxDigital uses Unbounce, obviously the results can be seen on our two websites, FlexxDigital and Flexxable.

But we also use the tool to create sales funnels for our clients. In previous chapters, I've spoken about creating an ad in the Facebook platform, then building an advertorial, a lander and a thank you page. The process for all of these has been explained to you in the book so far.

However, I understand that you may be feeling nervous about building advertorials and landers that look good enough to convert prospects into high-quality leads.

Having been in that situation myself, I've decided to give you the funnels we use right here, in this book.

Yes, really.

So, I would recommend, if you haven't done already, going onto the Unbounce site and signing up for a free trial.

Unbounce contains extensive instructions and video tutorials showing you how to use the website. I would recommend the following.

- **Get Started with Unbounce -** A quick, no-nonsense guide to diving right in
- **The Unbounce Anatomy -** Get an extensive overview of your new split-testing and high-converting workhorse of a webpage builder
- **Working With the Unbounce Builder -** Grasp the essential basics of designing a page using Unbounce
- **Getting Your Leads -** Learn how to capture and collect your leads
- **Unbounce Community -** Sign up to the community forum to converse with, question, and connect with hordes of Unbounce users

When you've explored the site and feel a bit more comfortable, take a look at the advertorial, landing page (or "lander"), and thank you page templates we'll provide for you.

Once you have these templates, you'll be able to take those files, upload them into your new Unbounce account, then alter the content to match the product or service your company offers.

These templates will give you an advantage over other businesses struggling to generate leads. Over the years, I have spent literally millions of dollars on producing traffic for these pages, so I know what works. I also know what looks good and what Facebook's algorithm desperately wants to see.

After months of split-testing and trialling hundreds of designs and features, we know *exactly what converts.*

The Big Advantage of Using Unbounce

One of the major advantages of Unbounce is the ability to install your advertorials and landing pages directly on your websites as subdomains.

This feature will save hundreds of dollars and thousands of hours.

The conversion platform's other assets include:

- Enabling you to have full control and access to all your pages, so you can make changes at any time
- Stopping you having to send traffic to a webpage that isn't designed to convert leads
- The ability to design and publish the pages without having to wait for your "web developer" to find time in his schedule
- The ability to run split-tests easily on different pages

Just these reasons alone make Unbounce absolutely invaluable.

Unbounce and GDPR

Unbounce is fully GDPR compliant. To find out more, please enter www.unbounce.com/gdpr/ into your browser and visit the page *Unbounce: a fully GDPR compliant platform.* There you will find all your questions answered when it comes to the following topics:

- Data storage
- Data Protection Officers
- The Right to Erasure
- Cookies
- The Lawful Basis of Processing
- Deletion (leads)
- The Data Processing Agreement (DPA)
- Security
- How to make your landing pages GDPR compliant

With the proper use of this site, the marketing world will be your oyster. The Unbounce platform has been explicitly designed for website conversion, going to great lengths to ensure marketing teams can focus on creating, publishing and measuring campaigns without any coding.

I'm going to stop beating around the bush. Turn the page for access to your Unbounce template links and watch all your doubts just melt away. These templates transformed my business, and I know they'll do the same for yours.

Building Advertorials and Landing Pages

And here they are, the templates you've all been waiting for.

https://bit.ly/2q38uKj

Just type this shortened link into your browser, and you'll find a zip file containing three blank templates: an advertorial, a landing page and a thank you page.

When you've opened the link, it'll direct you to a Google Drive page. Just click the download icon in the upper-right hand corner, and the zip file will appear in your download list.

If you're struggling to open or upload any of these files, please email us at support@flexxable.com. One of our staff will help you within 24 hours.

Applying the Unbounce Campaign Templates

This bit is extremely easy, which is why Unbounce is such a joy to work with.

1. Copy and paste the link into your browser. This should open in a new tab.

2. Right click and download the file, but **DO NOT** open it yet. If you try and open the file, **you will corrupt it.**

3. Head over to Unbounce and upload the ".unbounce" file you've just downloaded. If you're using an Apple Mac rather than a PC, use the built-in unzip tool to extract the ".unbounce" files before uploading them to the platform.

Warning: Make sure the file name has no special characters, such as brackets. There should only be letters, underscores and numbers.

If you download more than once, you'll get brackets like this in the file name: *Name of Document* (1).

If you try and upload a file with brackets, the template will not work. So, be careful!

Making The Templates Your Own

Once you've uploaded your templates, Unbounce makes it very easy for you to make any changes. You can add or remove elements on the page to suit your needs, switch images and text, and adjust any colours or fonts to match your brand's look and feel.

It's also crucial that you create mobile versions of your pages once you've got the desktop versions perfected. If you use Unbounce's Layout Assistant tool, it'll get your mobile page 80% publish-ready. Then you can tinker with the remaining page elements and resize your text to the appropriate size. Better yet, if you've got something on the site you don't want on the mobile page, you've got the option to hide it.

Unbounce will even offer the option to choose whether you want your page to be visible on search engines. It'll help you to optimise the information with a keyword-focused page title, a meta description, and which action you'd like to track as a conversion.

Setting Your Pages' URLs

Once you've finished your page, you'll need to launch it. Unbounce allows you to publish your page to the domain of your choice and customise the URL to fit your needs.

Adding the finished page to your domain is absolutely essential. If a customer clicked your ad on Facebook and was directed to a unbouncepages.com website, all the effort you've put into choosing the right photos, writing the best copy and creating beautiful pages would go to waste. Your audience would spot the difference in domain names and would assume you weren't a legitimate site. As with everything, credibility is vital.

On the back of this, make sure your new Unbounce pages match the message you're conveying in your advertisements. People love consistency and are very sensitive to sudden changes in tone, style or even image choice. If your landing page looks completely different to your Facebook ad or advertorial, you may be shutting the door on potential customers.

Finally, a mismatched URL can be a massive waste of money. Remember Chapter 4, when I talked about Facebook's relevance score? Determined to keep "fake news" or "click bait" to minimum levels, the social media platform has become hyper-vigilant when it comes to weeding out time-wasters. Your ad may be rejected from the outset or forced so far down the Facebook relevance ladder that it will appear on far fewer newsfeeds than you'd like.

For such a simple change, it's not worth the risk.

Adding Tracking and Custom Scripts

Unbounce's Script Manager allows you to embed scripts like Google Analytics, AdWords or any other custom code to multiple pages at once. You can't do this with an unbouncepages.com link, so make sure you've definitely changed your URL.

Unbounce has all the information to add a script to your page.

1. **Click on Settings** in the lefthand menu
2. **Click on Script Manager**
3. **Add your script** (or, if you've used the script before, click on the Add Script button at the top of the screen)
4. **Enter a name for your script** and **click the green Add Script Details button**
5. Use the **first** drop-down menu to **choose the placement of your script**
6. Use the **second** drop-down menu to select whether you want your script added to your **main pages, confirmation dialog pages, or both**
7. **Paste your script into the editor window**
8. **Choose the domains you'd like to add your script to** (you can see the list on the right)
9. **Click on the Save Changes button** at the bottom left of the screen

Unbounce will apply your script to all pages for the chosen domain, and will also refer it automatically to all new pages added to the same domain.

Integrating Your Page with the Facebook Pixel

1. **Go to the Pixels Section of Facebook Ads Manager and click Set Up Pixel**
2. **Click Manually Install the Code Yourself**
3. Scroll down to **Copy The Entire Pixel Code and Paste It In The Website Header,** then **copy the entire pixel code**
4. In the Unbounce Builder, select the **Javascript tab** and **paste the pixel code** in the script field

5. Click **Head** for placement, then **Save Code**
6. Click **Form Confirmation Dialog,** select the **Javascript** tab, and **paste the code again**
7. Click **Head** for placement, then **Save Code**
8. Well done. Your pixel will now track visits to every page where the pixel code exists

Adding a Lead Conversion

1. Go to the **Pixels Section** of Facebook Ads Manager and click **Set Up Pixel**
2. Click **Manually Install the Code Yourself**
3. Click **Continue**
4. Click **Generate Lead** and **select the code** to copy it to the clipboard
5. In the Unbounce Builder**, click Form Confirmation Dialog**
6. Select the **Javascript** tab and select the javascript that contains the pixel code you inserted in **Adding a Facebook Pixel**
7. Press **Enter** after **fbq('track,'"PageView");** and **paste the event code**
8. On the screen, you'll see numbered lines of code**. Delete** the **two extra Script tabs** and click **Save Code**
9. Select **Head** for placement and click **Save Code**

Once all that's done, preview your pages on both your desktop *and* your mobile and ensure that it looks as good as you want it to. Once you're happy, simply press **Publish.**

You can also use Google Tag Manager for managing your pixel. That's a whole new chapter, but it's a super user-friendly tool for running your tags (the snippets of JavaScript that sends information to third parties) on your website or mobile. For more information on GTM, please see the Google Developers page at: https://developers.google.com/tag-manager/.

Duplicating Your Pages

Now that the hard work is done, you can scale up production by duplicating your pages and making adjustments suitable for your various campaigns.

Duplication is really helpful for when you want to split test your advertorials, landers or thank you pages and see which layout and style resonate most with your audience. This is a quick little process and, in just a couple of minutes, you can split traffic across the two variants and find the one with the highest conversion rate.

1. Access the **Pages** tab, which will show you a list of your Unbounce pages
2. Then access the **Gear Menu** of the page you want to duplicate and select **Duplicate Page**
3. Select the Page Variants and features you'd like to copy using the checkboxes in the **Duplicate** dialog window
4. Click **Duplicate Page**
5. The new page will appear in the **Pages** tab, along with the others. This duplicated page is independent of the original and can be edited separately

Happy creating!

Conclusion

Learn To Fly

Social media isn't a tactic. You can plan and plan and plan some more, all with a specific end in mind. And, just when you think you've mapped out the perfect path, a colleague steps on an unmarked landmine.

You have to learn to roll with the punches. Facebook's algorithms change all the time. You hear about new tweaks and "slight changes" and, the next thing you know, everyone is lounging in a pit of despair.

I know how that feels. Every development and "new feature" is like the end of the world, and I worry about shutting FlexxDigital down four or five times a year.

The costs per leads are spiking.

We lose money.

But I've found that when things aren't going well, they always have a way of sorting themselves out.

To succeed in social marketing and lead generation, companies need to learn how to relinquish control. Social media is a catalogue of online testimonials, customer experiences, and opinion pieces. You, as a business, will need to learn how to welcome all this - the good, the bad and, unfortunately, the ugly - and promote positive customer interactions. Invite the feedback. Comment on conversations about your product or service. Social media isn't just about your marketing department - it impacts everything from production to the paperwork.

You need to learn to fly. Take your ideas and run with them. Always strive to be the best, even if it means making some changes that could put you under strain.

In the rise of the digital age, some industries are really feeling the pinch. In the Western World, newspaper publishing employment rate has dropped by 45.5%.

Telephone apparatus manufacturers have sunk by 48.6%.

Libraries are closing, DVD retail stores are shutting down by the day. The touch of nostalgia in me feels sad about this, as if we're losing touch with the past.

The truth of the matter is, technology has brought a new wave of efficiency. In 500 years time, what we've left behind won't matter, and our economy will fare far better for the gains in productivity.

To keep up, you need to be continually deploying new features, learning about current trends and coming up with innovative ideas. The big companies, like Facebook and Google, are updating themselves constantly. They are, as I've said to do with your own ad strategies, always *failing fast and sorting the problem even faster.* They know when to hold up their hands and say they've made mistakes, but they keep on going and continue to sail into uncharted waters. And, as a result, they're never left behind.

They've made it easier for you to keep up too.

I have shared with you my secrets when it comes to generating leads. I have shown you how to create and build campaigns, what makes a fail-proof sales funnel, how to leverage your newfound powers to find prospects on Facebook, command their attention, capture their details, nurture their trust and turn them into happy customers.

You now have a whole armoury of tactics, tips and templates to make a game plan, up it, and then change the entirety of the game forever.

For the last few years, I have generated leads for companies big and small, designed their landing pages and helped them to achieve their maximum potential. In the introduction, I told you that I've now made it my mission to help companies take their advertising and marketing in-house.

I hope, in this book, I've accomplished that and more. What you have read is a guide to the success that lies in your hands, not those of a third party. You can create all this largely on your own.

For Further Help...

However, if you still feel like you need some help or extra clarification, don't hesitate to ask. Make your way over to my site, flexxable.com. Here, you will find a quiz that'll guide you towards the extra training you need. We'd be really happy to have you.

I believe we can all make our stories bigger and better. See you at the top, and let me know how you get on!